P9-DEP-029

J. I. BIEGELEISEN
Instructor, New York School of Industrial Art

GREENBERG : PUBLISHER • NEW YORK

Second printing before publication,
December, 1945.

Printed in the United States of America

PREFACE

My heartfelt thanks go to the following artists and art directors who so graciously lent their assistance in the preparation of this book. The readiness with which all responded was gratifying proof that a book on poster design was needed. I hope that this text will fill that need and that it will not prove disappointing to those who showed faith in the undertaking and the author.

Lester Beall, Jean Carlu, McKnight Kauffer, Sascha Maurer, Leslie Ragan, Howard Simon, Henry Stahlhut, Alex Steinweiss, Carl Woerner, Sidney Asp of Columbia Recording Corporation, Al Cadiff of American Display Company, John Elsey of McCann-Erickson, Miss Rose Gandel of Russian War Relief, Dr. Goris of Belgian Information Center, Sidney Herbert of Poster Division of OWI, Miss Hollis of Bloomingdale's, Jesse Kram of Kram Advertising, Miss Long of British Ministry of Information, Raymond Martin of Consolidated Edison Company, C. D. McCormick of Outdoor Advertising Incorporated, F. S. McGinnis of Southern Pacific Company, Mark Seelan of Outdoor Advertising Incorporated, Walter Soderstrom of National Association of Photo-Lithographers, and Arthur Werback of Abraham and Straus.

J. I. Biegeleisen

April 1945

CONTENTS

CHAPTER ONE

POSTER DESIGNING AS A CAREER

HERALDING the 1945 Red Cross contribution campaign was a poster that you surely remember. How can anyone who has seen it, forget it? The design featured a blue-black background with a white arrow pointing diagonally downward to the simple one-word message GIVE. The small red cross in the white arrow was the focal color spot. In the lower right-hand corner in unobtrusive lettering was the artist's signature: E. McKnight Kauffer. Millions of copies of this poster were printed in a variety of different sizes and dimensions. They were distributed for posting on wall panels, sides of trucks, bulletin boards in schools, churches, and public buildings, in the interiors of trains, busses, and surface cars, in store windows, and on the giant outdoor bulletins on highways and busy thoroughfares. This design, no doubt, was a potent factor in achieving the overwhelming public response to the Red Cross appeal for funds.

What about the creator of this memorable design? Who is E. McKnight Kauffer and what is his specialized business? Kauffer is one of thousands of artists whose job it is to design posters. People like him, whose names are well known to artists and advertisers on two continents, don't have much breathing time between orders. They are busy as can be all the year 'round, and are handsomely paid for their creative efforts. One famous poster artist whose designs appear regularly on car cards and subway billboards holds a lifetime contract with a large chewing gum company. His income permits him to live on an island of his own with all the attendant luxuries of a Hollywood movie star. Not every poster artist can afford private island possessions, but any man or woman who can actively participate in the creation of a poster can always count on a good livelihood. Poster art is definitely excluded from the category of "the starving arts." There are even newcomers, just beginning to make a name for themselves, who are already earning over 250 dollars a week. One in particular—a young chap under thirty who in all modesty does not compare himself to men like Kauffer, Bernhard, Carlu, Binder, or other great contemporaries—makes about 1000 dollars a week. He could earn more if there were more than twenty-four hours to the day.

The most prominent artists work in their own studios as free lancers. They do this because of the freedom of working habits it allows them and also because they cannot expect to be paid on a straight salary basis as much as they can earn "on their own." An unattached artist is free to take on only those assignments which he will enjoy doing and for which he will, at the same time, be paid what he considers a fair price. Staff artists, who work on a regular salary basis, usually prefer a steady job even if it means a less-spectacular earning capacity.

Many free lancers augment their incomes with commissions not strictly within the scope of poster design, but which call for the same basic skills. Take that busy young man who averages 1000 dollars a week. He designs posters for outdoor billboards and car cards. He also does magazine covers and layouts for cosmetic advertising. His versatility is surpassed by one of the foremost commercial artists in America who is as well known for his printing of type faces, package designs, and trademarks as for his distinctive posters. Another poster artist has made a phenomenal success as a designer of decorative record albums. Still another divides his time between poster and book-jacket designs. Only the fact that these artists have had a well-rounded preparation in all the basic art skills makes it possible for them to tackle these diversified assignments. After all, the common denominator of all design and composition is good taste. Designing is mainly a matter of applying good taste and discretion while stressing the particular element which best fulfills the specific objective of the design. The elements of good design are fundamentally the same in any graphic composition.

The designing and production of posters has become a thriving business profitable to the owners and remunerative also to those engaged as staff artists. It is a good field for steady employment because it can offer a place to each person, commensurate with his ability. There are shops and studios which turn out only theatrical posters; some which vie with each other for the cleaning store trade; others which specialize in three-dimensional display designing—where special displays and decorative poster panels are designed, constructed, and painted.

There is a firm in New York City for instance, which has made a specialty of theatrical posters and displays. Three floors in a large building are already devoted to this work and additional space is needed to handle the ever increasing volume of business. This business operates under a division-of-labor plan whereby each man on the staff is a specialist doing only the one part of the job which he can do best. This is how it works out. There is a "hand work department" where show cards, posters, and signs are painted by hand in small quantities. The minimum union wage for this work is $16.75 per eight-hour day—and union membership is a prerequisite of employment. Then there is the silk screen printing department, set up under a similar division of tasks. The rough layout of the art work is sketched in by the senior artist of the department. The illustration is handled by an artist who is especially proficient in painting the type of scenes or portraits used on movie posters. It is his job to render the art work in the flat technique suitable for silk screen reproduction. When this part of the job is finished, the poster is passed on to the lettering specialist. Neither collaborator, of course, deviates from the original layout. When OK'd by the higher-ups in the front office, the finished poster is acknowledged ready for printing. It is given to the stencil artist who plans the order of colors and prepares the printing plates. It is the job of the printing foreman to supervise the printing, check on color proofs, and see that the work gets out according to schedule.

The setup in this company is not at all unusual. There are other and bigger shops devoted to the production of theatrical posters and displays. There are also many smaller studios where the same kind of work is done and where all sorts of show cards, streamers, and signs are produced. There are art and display studios in most large department stores where a person skilled in poster art or in one phase of it will find opportunity for employment. Advertising departments of chain store organizations likewise have their own poster divisions where posters are conceived and produced. In these smaller establishments, where the personnel is limited, one employee may be called upon to make himself useful in more than one way and thus can get a wide range of experience.

Poster designs with the widest circulation are conceived in the big advertising agencies, usually by top-notch artists working on a free-lance basis. The best art available is bought; the artist's fee for this kind of work ranges from 150 dollars to 1000 dollars. But it is easy to see how the cost of the art work is relatively unimportant when it is compared to the expense entailed in the large-scale production of the posters.

The art director distributes the assignments so that each artist does the work for which he is best known. He may call in a famous man who excels in a certain painting technique and tell him to confine himself to the illustration part of the poster as indicated in the rough layout. Another artist will be assigned to do the lettering. If one artist could do the entire job, that would suit the art director better, but there are far too few men he can call upon who excel in both illustration and lettering. A happy professional destiny is in store for the artist whose background and experience will prepare him to handle the complete job. But it will take special preparation.

Just how intense the training should be, depends on one's ambition. Obviously it takes less training to learn one specific skill than it does to acquire a mastery of a wider field. If a perusal of the want ad columns can be taken as a valid index, the most sought after skill in all commercial art occupations seems to be lettering ability. Many of our famous contemporary poster artists started out as letterers.

A formal art school education will be found helpful—though not indispensable. Ludwig Hohlwein, the dean of modern poster designers, had no formal art training whatever. He is not a lone oddity in this respect. There are others. Cassandre, the great French designer, is another self-trained man. Attendance at a school is no assurance of success. Art schools are sending out an endless procession of graduates equipped with plenty of superficial academic theories but with pitifully little practical experience. Since it is an indisputable axiom that we learn by doing, it goes without saying that actual practice is the thing that counts—not a "Cook's Tour" through the maze of subjects listed under fancy names in school catalogues. Courses of a practical nature in lettering, design and composition, perspective, color, freehand drawing, and anatomy are useful.

Many an artist now famous, got his start by serving a humble apprenticeship with a busy artist. These men will tell you that there is no learning device quite so helpful in getting started and in evolving proper professional attitudes as that of working under a "master."

Whether the learner receives his training in the sheltered atmosphere of an art school or under the watchful eye of the Master, poster art—though only one branch of the larger field of commercial art—offers fertile ground for professional growth. Employment opportunities are good, and there is such a division of skills that there is room for practically any serious-minded person to make this a permanent life's work. How much preparation it will take depends upon your intended specialty, the source of instruction, and you.

CHAPTER TWO

HOW IT ALL BEGAN

OUR history of poster art begins in the 1870's. It begins with the work of the French poster designers Cheret, Steinlen, and Toulouse-Lautrec. Although signs, trademarks, and other commercial designs have been used for centuries, poster art as we know it today did not emerge as a distinct form until the last lap of the nineteenth century.

Inscriptions, signs, and posters share a common historical heritage. Broadly speaking, the art of pictorial design can be traced back to remote antiquity, to the early attempts of man to record (by means of painted or incised pictures) his impressions of the daily events of his harried existence. In the absence of a formal language, a picture or symbol became a ready vehicle of expression. Records remain which stand out as mute evidence of the urge of even the most primitive of the human species to grope for articulation through drawing. The work of the primitive artist was prompted, in the main, by this desire for self-expression, and indirectly served as a pictorial diary of his thoughts, activities, and superstitions.

On the rugged walls of his abode, the cave dweller projected his impressions of the gods he worshipped and feared; he recorded his prowess as a warrior, and his supremacy over bird and beast. These wall decorations may be classed as posters, if the purpose of a poster is merely to convey a thought through conscious design. The narrower concept of poster art, however, limits the definition of a poster to a publicly-displayed design that is intended for commerce and industry. It therefore becomes an academic question whether or not the creative endeavors of the cave dwellers should be alluded to as poster art.

Scanning the cavalcade of centuries as we approach the Christian era, we begin to find in the art of the Assyrians, Babylonians, Egyptians, Greeks, and Romans, something which approximates the poster form as we know it today. Fragmentary wall excavations from the petrified ashes of Pompeii disclose the fact that art in those days served more than as a graphic record of events and impressions; posters had become a widely used medium for disseminating specific information to the populace. In ancient Greece, outdoor posters were displayed at market places, in the Forum, and wherever else people were wont to gather, announcing new laws and bearing other public proclamations. Roman signboards advertised coming gladiatorial contests, public baths, theatrical performances, and slave marts, and featured other announcements reflecting the interests and activities of the time.

With the rise of Christianity came the extended use of signs and posters as a means of spreading the Gospel. The blessings of Heaven and the curse of Hell became very real to the illiterate, who learned the teachings of Christianity not only through inspired sermons, but also through dramatized pictures on walls and banners.

After civilization's slumber through the Dark Ages, came the Renaissance period, with its renewed intellectual activity and its corresponding revival of commerce and industry. In the competition for trade, merchants inaugurated the custom of distributing advertising handbills and displaying posters and signs in busy thoroughfares. Picturesque signboards bearing trademarks and inscriptions were put up to identify the silversmith, the apothecary, the innkeeper, and other business establishments.

As an intellectual curio, it may be of interest to note that advertising took on another form at about this time. The town crier, forerunner of the modern radio announcer, came into being. In a melodious chant the town crier sang the praises of his sponsor's wares as he carried his portly figure through the narrow streets of Paris and London. After a while, this practice became so widespread that it was necessary to pass legislation regulating the activities of these hundreds of walking advertisements.

The year 1440 is of special significance in the history of poster making. Prior to this time, the quantity of posters and signs that could be produced was limited to the number that could be painted by hand or printed from hand-cut woodblocks or stencils. With the invention of movable type, the complexion of advertising was changed from a limited output to quantity production. Whereas the exact year of the discovery of movable type will forever remain a matter of dispute among historians and printing authorities, we shall not enter the controversy here, but accept 1440 as the year in which Johann Gutenberg revealed to the people of Mainz and to the world at large, the astonishingly simple fact that the various characters of the alphabet could be cut in separate little blocks and spaced together to compose words and sentences. Heretofore, an entire page of reading matter was cut out of and printed from a single woodblock. The block, which took much time and great skill to cut, became useless after the edition for which it was intended was completed. Individual type units comprising the letters of the alphabet, Gutenberg demonstrated, could be re-used and re-combined indefinitely. This idea raised printing from the level of an artist's tedious handicraft to that of a practical commercial process. The introduction of movable type and the subsequent development and improvement in printing presses had an immeasurable effect on culture and civilization, advancing at the same time the technique of poster reproduction.

In 1796, with the discovery of the lithographic process by Alois Senefelder, the production of posters in color was further advanced. Though designs could be reproduced in color with hand-cut woodblocks and stencils (indeed, many fine examples remain to attest to that art), the lithographic process could do the job better and without the limitations inherent in the stencil or woodblock. Further developments which came about with the introduction of zinc plates, photo offset, three- and four-color process, and so forth, freed poster artists from the remaining technical restrictions as to style, technique, and range of colors.

Let us turn from our brief historical excursion and recount the evolution of modern poster design through the achievements of the outstanding personalities that helped to shape its development.

In 1866, Jules Cheret, an artist and mural painter, returned to Paris from a stay in England where he had studied lithographic processes. Upon his return, this craftsman set himself up as a designer and printer of posters. He was a self-taught artist who found in Japanese art the secret of good poster design—flat colors applied with a stencil-like effect, eliminating inconsequentials in the subject matter, and striving chiefly for a pleasing design. The Japanese two-dimensional style influenced his sense of design, but for his color inspiration he turned to French Impressionism. The colors on Cheret posters had a spectral purity and vibrant intensity entirely suitable to the sparkling personality of the theatrical characters he depicted. His subject matter, dealing mainly with the gaieties of Parisian night life in theaters and cafes, was audacious and full of merriment, but never passed the bounds of propriety. Among his earliest designs was a poster made in 1867, announcing the appearance of the immortal Sarah Bernhardt. All in all, he produced more than a thousand poster designs. He was in perfect control of the medium because he understood the possibilities of the lithographic process and had the facilities for doing his own printing. Cheret posters began to attract attention, not only to the things they advertised, but also to themselves as works of art. All of Paris began to look forward to the next Cheret poster, and took a deep pride in these designs that so colorfully decorated the advertising kiosks.

By 1880, this new art form had attracted other designers. Alexandre Steinlen and Toulouse-Lautrec followed to a great extent the established pattern of Cheret. The subject matter of their posters was essentially the same—devoted to advertising the night life, frivolity, and colorful splendor of the music halls and cabarets of gay Paris. Lautrec, who was not so prolific as Cheret, but who was perhaps the better draftsman, exerted a tremendous influence on other poster designers. By 1900, more than two hundred artists in Paris were experimenting with the new poster technique. George Meunier, Pierre Bonnard, Alphonse Mucha, Eugene Grasset, and Adolphe Willette stood out from among the rest.

The work of the French designers had a stimulating effect on the comparatively drab poster art of England. In a poster exhibition in England in 1894, the French influence was noticeably reflected in the work of Aubrey Beardsley, Will Owen, Dudley Hardy, Walter Crane, James Pryde, and William Nicholson. The last-named two collaborated on poster designs under the pseudonym of "The Beggarstaff Brothers." They were designers who set out to prove how striking a poster can be in simple flat areas and limited to few colors. No attempt was made at realism. Their designs represented frank statements of the two-dimensional limitations of paint applied on a flat plane, and gave the illusion of colored paper cutouts pasted in a harmonious composition. This illusion was quite understandable, for it was precisely that cutout technique which the Beggarstaffs often employed in designing their posters.

The Beggarstaffs, as well as Aubrey Beardsley and other British designers, in turn inspired American poster art. It is said that Beardsley's effect on the American, William Bradley, was so marked that the latter became known as the American Beardsley. Edward Penfield, too, fell under the Beardsley spell. Among other notable early American designers whose work is still seen or whose influence is still felt are F. G. Cooper, C. B. Falls, H. M. Meyers, C. E. Millard, Harrison Fisher, and Adolph Treidler.

Influenced somewhat by this new poster art movement, but not yielding to it entirely, was the individual style of the German artist Ludwig Hohlwein. Hohlwein was an advertising artist with an avid interest in hunting and sports. His technique was a strange blending of East-Asiatic simplicity with the photographic accuracy of a snapshot. He was a master in the portrayal of the figures of man and beast, and he achieved the effect of great detail through clever suggestion rather than by actual delineation. He omitted all nonessentials and made adroit use of strong patches of shadows contrasted with crisp gleaming flashes of highlights. His genius was recognized throughout Germany and by artists and advertisers the world over.

Among others who added to the prestige of German poster design were Paul Scheurich, H. R. Erdt, and Lucian Bernhard. Bernhard sought his inspiration from the experimental abstract form developed by the great Austrian poster artist Julius Klinger. In that, Bernhard differed from his German colleagues who, under the spell of Hohlwein, produced poster designs that had become increasingly illustrative and realistic. Bernhard was the first of the German commercial artists to popularize the rugged and stark simplicity of abstract form. His Priester Match poster, known to every student of poster design, remains a legendary model of dramatic simplicity.

The work of Joseph Binder represents another distinct approach to poster design. His illustrations have a two-dimensional quality, with details sacrificed to design. Instead of emphasizing the abstract or grotesque, Binder builds up his illustrative material with simple colorful shapes, creating a geometrical pattern of design. He is the exponent of the theory of "harmony of color contrasts," a working philosophy of daring color combination which was adopted by artists in Austria where Binder originally worked, and spread as a gospel to other countries. Sascha Maurer, another Viennese now in America, has done commendable work, carrying on this tradition of abstract design, but compromising with shades of realism. His famous skiing posters are always dynamic in composition, conveying a feeling entirely suitable to the spirit of sports.

Leon Bakst of Russia, H. Cassiers of Belgium, and Toyokuni of Japan have brought distinction to the poster art of their respective countries.

The Underground Railway System of Great Britain has been one of the most important patrons of poster art in England. Their travel posters have always been executed with such picturesque appeal that it has become popular with the poorer people to purchase these posters as wall decorations for their homes. The lettering is usually so placed that the advertising matter can be blocked out or cut away without marring the general effect of the composition. Heading the group of outstanding designers of England is McKnight Kauffer, an American by birth, who established his professional reputation in England. Among others of repute are Austin Cooper, Fred Taylor, Tom Purvis, Pat Keely, and A. Games.

After the first World War, France, the original source of poster inspiration (as indeed of all progressive art movements), recovered the glory of Cheret through the refreshingly new poster techniques of A. M. Cassandre, Jean Carlu, Charles Loupot, and others of that experimental school. They relied more on symbolism and on a free decorative motif than on literal interpretation of subject matter. Cassandre's work, in particular, shows a leaning to the new art movements borrowed from the Monet and Manet and Picasso schools of modern painting. These French poster artists are designers, not illustrators, as are so many of our American poster artists.

In America, poster art is not founded on the elements of pure design so typical of poster treatment in Europe. It has always leaned toward anecdotal illustration. From this point of view, we have fallen behind Germany, England, and France in the competition—some critics assert that we were never in the race. Our work, they maintain, is insipid, unimaginative, and devoid of good taste. The typical American poster consists of a sensational illustration crowded out by a mass of lettering. We are not design-conscious; we are too preoccupied with the movies to bother much with pictures that do not flicker. Even our posters "play to the gallery." We excel in technique, speed, and fidelity of reproduction—especially in speed. In most European countries, advertising poster displays constitute outdoor museums, and the names of the poster artists are almost as familiar to the general public as are the names of movie stars to the American public. Poster exhibits are of interest not only to artists; they have a wide cultural appeal to the average man, also.

But the defenders of American poster design remind us that the poster is not an end in itself; it is a means to an end. The aim of the advertiser, bluntly expressed, is to sponsor a poster design which will zoom the sale of his product. Thus the acid test of a poster is its selling record. The efficacy of a poster is measured statistically. It is astonishing what quantities of beer, cigarettes, and toothpaste a realistic likeness of a glamour girl with a bewitching smile can sell. Sales, sales, sales—that's what the advertiser is paying for. The agencies show that this type of poster brings tangible results, and they prove it through ever-climbing sales charts.

American poster design at present is on a higher art level than formerly. This is due in large measure to the fact that many of the great designers of the world are now part of the American scene. Bayer, Bernhard, Binder, Carlu, and Kauffer—to name but a few—have set up their studios in New York and other large cities. It cannot but follow that their influence will emerge as a potent force in a changing concept of American poster design. Time will prove what Europeans have long known—that good design is not a handicap to the selling efficacy of a poster.

CHAPTER THREE

HOW GOOD IS YOUR LETTERING?

IT WOULD take a stroke of genius to create so expressive a pictorial design for a poster that no lettering at all would be required. Even then it is doubtful whether such a design, no matter how masterfully conceived, would satisfy the American advertiser. The average American advertiser cannot bear to see any paid-for space go to waste. He is a glutton when it comes to "copy."

The ironical thing about the advertiser's insatiable appetite for words is that most artists dislike to do lettering, and some flee from it entirely, leaving the half-finished poster on the doorstep of a specialist in that branch of art. The erroneous conception prevails that lettering is something that can be tagged onto a picture. It is, therefore, a fairly established habit with large art studios and agencies to divide the work of poster making between an illustrator and a letterer. The results, or rather, the consequences of such a coalition do not often prove artistically compatible. They make one strongly suspect that the two artists never even discussed the thing. Indeed, the twain may never have met. Often the illustrator does not see the finished poster until it has been printed and he is handed a press sheet for his files.

Poster art reduced to such a division-of-labor formula does not have the same singleness of effect as that in which one artist does both the illustration and the lettering. In the best tradition of poster design, as exemplified by the superb poster art of Hohlwein, F. G. Cooper, Lucian Bernhard, Hans Flato, and people of that caliber, the lettering carries the same stamp of individuality as the rest of the poster. The lettering is, in fact, an inseparable element of the design scheme.

Assuming that one is interested in poster design (in doing the entire job, not just the illustration), one should devote time to the study of lettering. Lettering does not come "easy"; it takes practice, patience, and precision. It is an objective kind of art where every stroke counts. Before attempting to do the type of lettering deemed good enough for a well-designed poster, one should learn how to do simple unadulterated brush lettering. Nothing fancy, just the unpretentious type of freehand lettering used on a show card.

It takes months (we are inclined to add quietly, years), to master the lettering brush to a stage where you can manipulate it with ease and assurance and shape the letter forms with an economy of strokes. Basic training consists in practicing the elementary strokes—straight, diagonal, and curved—and then combining the strokes to form the one-thickness letters of the Gothic alphabet. After acquiring experience with the Gothic alphabet, the learner is ready to experiment with lettering that is constructed on the thick-and-thin principle. He will discover that with sensitive variations in pressure the same brush is capable of producing strokes of varied thicknesses. This practice is orientation for the thick-and-thin letter forms of the Roman alphabet.

These first two practice styles should be attempted with a "one-stroke" technique. Each stroke should be made with one sweep of the brush, avoiding "going over" or "doctoring" imperfections. Such directness leads to the precision and manual discipline so necessary for facility in letter construction. When this rather rigid training period is up, the student is ready for the type of lettering known as "built-up." This means that the elements of the letters may be made in two or three strokes, to give definition of thickness and finish to the letter form. All this is preparatory for the final phase of lettering suitable for reproduction. This basic training should accomplish two things: it should provide all the wrist and finger exercises so essential to the art of freehand lettering, and should also provide a working analysis of the anatomy of lettering. The hardest part is over. The transition of skill from brush to other lettering tools is an easy one.

Lettering for reproduction should be based on a knowledge of freehand lettering. The manipulation of the ruling pen and compasses, being a mechanical procedure, requires but little practice. In the hands of a capable letterer these tools will be reserved for work in which mechanical precision is absolutely required. Instruments are not substitutes for the lettering brush or pen, and it is a serious mistake to rely on them too much. Lettering authorities agree that a mechanical instrument should be an aid, not a crutch.

The preparation thus far described equips one with the knowledge and skills of basic lettering. This background may be enriched through an analytical study of the history and development of letter forms traced to current alphabet styles and by an appreciation of the inherent possibilities of lettering as creative design. In his professional work an artist need not have an elaborate repertory of many styles. Though there are dozens of styles and an infinite number of variations, most artists have a few favorites on which they depend most of the time. All styles are derived from the following lettering families:

1. ROMAN—This style traces its classical origin to the beautiful lettering inscribed on the Trajan Column. It is a thick-and-thin letter with hairline terminals, called serifs. In the common parlance of letterers all thick-and-thin alphabets, whether they have serifs or not, are classed as Roman.

2. GOTHIC—In the same loose terminology of hand-lettering this style refers to the block or single-thick alphabets where all strokes are of equal thickness. It may or may not have serifs, but it is made mostly without them. This letter family is more serviceable to the poster artist than the more graceful Roman, because the Gothic letters can be made bold and powerful.

3. TEXT—This refers to manuscript styles, of which Old English is the most popular. The calligraphic pen styles may be classed in this same category. Text letters have only limited use on a poster, inasmuch as legibility and simplicity are impaired through the ornamental scrolls and flourishes that characterize this style.

4. ITALICS OR SCRIPTS—These are the slanted letters. All scripts, both formal and personalized, fall into this category. The script letter, based on handwriting, allows for endless variations and lends itself to highly individualistic interpretations. The arbitrary distinction between scripts and italics is based on the terminal strokes that may or may not link the letters together. As a general rule, when the letters are joined together as in handwriting, the style is called Script. When each letter is separate, the style is called Italics.

In practicing lettering, use a good book on the subject and don't hesitate to copy from standard specimen charts. Don't give your early attempts any original twists. Not yet. Wait until you can at least make a reasonable facsimile of the model alphabets. Too often the beginner in lettering, as in fact in any type of art, is tempted to hide behind artful distortion to cover up his lack of experience. A man like Picasso can distort the human figure, but being a master of anatomy and an excellent draftsman, he does it wilfully and magnificently. To him distortion is not a subterfuge. Nor to Salvador Dali. It is all right for creative artists like these to have their heads above the clouds, but they also have both feet planted firmly on the ground. Lucian Bernhard, who has designed many graceful and classic typefaces, often uses rugged-edged unconventional letters on his posters, which may appear rough and unfinished to the untrained eye. He uses these intentionally, for a special effect—certainly not because he is incapable of producing the more conventional letter forms. Deviation from convention must be in good taste, and good taste can be cultivated only through study, practice, and critical appreciation.

The art of lettering takes in more than the manipulative skill to shape isolated letters. It includes a sense of proper space relationship, so that an even tone will result when letters are grouped into words and words into sentences.

It is the area created between adjacent letters, not the linear measure that separates them, that is important in spacing. Spacing, therefore, is visual, not mechanical. What creates the difficulty is the fact that the construction of our letter forms is such that some letters like *L*, *J*, and *T* are comparatively "open," while others like *M*, *N*, and *O* are "closed." If every letter were of the same construction, then spacing could be purely mechanical. It would be as simple as measuring off the distances between the slats of a fence. As it is, compensations have to be made to meet every possible combination of letters. The best approach to the problem of spacing is to think of the areas between adjacent letters as being filled with a liquid. With that analogy in mind, you should space letters so that the volume of liquid contained in these areas will be uniform. Thus an open letter, such as *L*, adjacent to another open letter, such as *T*, should be spaced closer together than an *I* next to an *N*.

Eventually one should be introduced to the fascinating study of calligraphy and personalized scripts. This lettering art, based on ecclesiastical manuscript writing, has recently been revived, and its commercial possibilities have already been tapped. Calligraphy, one of the most personal and charming of all creative lettering styles, is a blend between handwriting and lettering. There is no rigid type to follow, nothing to go by but good taste and the inspiring tradition of fine penmanship. Not being very legible, calligraphic lettering should be used with discretion on posters, where legibility is so important.

MECHANICAL LETTERING AIDS

Numerous lettering aids have been developed and placed at the disposal of the commercial artist. The poster artist might do well to know what these devices are and how they may be used to supplement his standard means of preparing lettering for a poster.

WEBER PROCESS—The Weber Process is an ingenious, patented method whereby any kind of hand lettering, type, or line drawing can, by photographic means, be made to undergo a multitude of variations from the original design. With this process a line of lettering can be reduced, enlarged, condensed, extended, curved around an arc, made into a connected all-over pattern, or otherwise altered. The versatility of possible effects, coupled with the moderate charge for the service, makes it a logical means of getting variations in a basic design, which would be costly and time-consuming if attempted by hand. This is a professional service made available to artists, printers, and typographers.

PHOTOMAGNETIC LETTERING—This is a professional service which makes available a library of special alphabets, each made with the precision of type, yet retaining the hand letterer's touch. The poster artist selects from the catalogue of exclusive typefaces whatever style appeals to him and makes a layout, indicating the size and arrangement of the copy he wants set up. He need not do any lettering at all.

The photomagnetic lettering idea consists of black and white individual letter units spaced and arranged in any manner desired and held in position on a magnetic plate. The artist's layout and type specifications are followed. The arrangement is photographed and the artist is sent perfect black and white photo proofs of the lettering. This system has two main advantages over the regular printer's type setup. First, the typefaces are comparatively exclusive. Then, also, there is no restriction as to the layout or arrangement of the copy. Lettering may be set around a circle, may be stagger-spaced, may be overlapped, and so forth.

CELLULOID OVERLAY LETTERS—This is a means whereby an artist can set up ready-made letter forms that correspond to standard printer's typefaces. Large art supply stores carry sets of these patented celluloid alphabets in a wide variety of type designs and in different sizes. A set is composed of individual celluloid squares, each one of which has a black opaque letter processed on its transparent surface. The individual letters can be spaced out and pasted on any cardboard or directly on the poster, all ready for the printer. This device does away with some of the hand lettering and the need of printer's proofs. In contrast to the Weber or Magnetic procedure, the art work doesn't have to leave the studio; the artist is in complete control of the entire operation. After the letters are used for one job, they may be taken off the poster and put away for re-use on another job.

WRICO LETTERING GUIDES—This mechanical lettering aid is popular with engineers and draftsmen who are notoriously poor hand letterers. The lettering guide consists of a long strip of thick celluloid, with openings cut in the shape of letters of the alphabet. An ink stylus is used to follow the contours of the letters as they are defined by the die-cut openings. The guide is shifted forward as each letter is made.

TYPE—The typesetter is the hand letterer's closest ally. It is the custom of many advertising agencies to relieve their overburdened art staff by having much of the routine lettering work set up in type. The usual procedure is for the illustrator to complete his painting and indicate on a tissue overlay the style, weight, size, and location of the lettering that would go well with the composition.

Neither type nor any mechanical or photographic device, no matter how ingenious, really threatens to supplant the hand letterer's art. There will never be a machine to do anything creative, whether in the sphere of art, literature, or music. A machine, a device, or a process can at best only reproduce or modify that which has been fed into it. There will never be a machine to write an "Ode to a Daffodil" or to compose another *New World Symphony*. There will never be a machine to design a poster or to create a lettering style. If such machines are ever made, then surely God's intentions will have been thwarted.

LETTERING TOOLS AND EQUIPMENT

You have probably heard it before. For the best results, get the best tools. Whatever the cost, it is but a small investment compared to what is at stake. Your professional experience will prove that to you.

Lettering Brush. The best type of all-round lettering brush is the one familiarly known as the show card brush. It has a round ferrule and sable hairs that come to a flat chisel edge. In a good lettering brush the bristles have a nice resilience and will spring back upon release of pressure.

Brushes are classed as medium, short, or long, depending upon the length of the bristles. It is of no great consequence which kind you get—merely a matter of preference. If your lettering experience has been so limited that you have not established any preference, it may be well to start your collection with a medium-sized one. Brushes are also classified according to the width of the chisel. They range in size from #1 to #20; the higher the number, the larger the brush. You do not need all numbers to get started. A #4, #8, and #12 should be ample. The #8 will be the busiest of the lot. It produces a stroke of convenient thickness for the kind of display letters used on posters. If used chisel edge without pressure, it makes a natural stroke of about one-quarter inch in width. Used sideways, it can produce an almost hairline stroke. Another type of lettering brush, known as the Rigger, tapers to a point and is reserved for script lettering, outlining, fine embellishments, and so forth.

We said before that a good brush is a good investment because it will serve you well, but the best of brushes can become a discipline problem if it is not accorded proper treatment. A show card lettering brush is made for use with tempera poster colors and should not be used with oil or Japan paints. It should never be used as a mixing mop for stirring paint. The brush should always be washed in cold water immediately after use, and be put away, bristle side up. Some brush fanciers go so far as to sprinkle moth flakes over the bristles to protect them from moths when the brush is not in use. Use the brush more than the moths do is perhaps better advice. Preserving the brush, commendable as that practice is, will not teach you to letter.

Lettering Pen. Pen and ink lettering is rarely used on posters because the pen has a tendency to scratch on a surface coated with paint, and the ink tends to run and blur. The lettering pen is designed for use with free-flowing ink on a smooth unpainted surface. Letterers will resort to pen work mostly for fine scripts, calligraphic styles, and black-on-white jobs designed for reproduction.

Instrument Set. For the execution of rigid styles, typelike in perfection, one should equip himself with several items from a standard draftsman's instrument set. The three most important items in the wide assortment of bric-a-brac usually found in such a set are the pencil bow compasses, the ink bow compasses, and the ruling pen. It is a better idea to purchase just these essential pieces and get the best, rather than to get a complete set of mediocre quality. The price you pay, assuming you patronize a reputable dealer, is a reasonably good index of the quality of the merchandise. Such, at least, is the trusting opinion of most honest people. Beware of "bargains" unless you are a shrewd trader and know quality when you see it.

The compasses may be used for constructing letters with predominantly round elements. It is not good practice to use the compasses for incidental rounded segments of a letter which could just as well be done freehand. The ruling pen is intended for straight strokes, for outlines, and for ruling borders. Both the ruling pen and the ink compasses will take ink as well as tempera color which has been properly diluted with water.

Guard against dropping any instrument, for a blunted ruling pen or bent compasses may require hours of patient nursing to be restored to usefulness. All instruments should be carefully cleaned after use.

T Square and Celluloid Triangle. The T square is an indispensable tool for squaring up art work and getting perpendicular and horizontal lines. There are two kinds. The standard T square, made of wood, steel, or plastic, is constructed with a fixed right-angle head rigidly attached to a perpendicular blade. The other type is so constructed that the head may be set to any arbitrary angle by means of a thumbscrew adjustment. This makes it easy to rule mechanically perfect diagonal lines running parallel to each other. Celluloid triangles, both the 30-60 degree type and the 45-degree type, are handy for squaring up and ruling in pencil and ink lines.

A metal-edged ruler, art gum, chamois cloth, and the usual equipment of the art studio are as necessary to the letterer as to the general commercial artist.

Let us pause here to make the acquaintance of an imaginary character in the person of a practicing artist. We shall join him now and at the end of every chapter hereafter for a Question and Answer session.

Q. Can you tell us how you know what style of lettering to put on a poster?

A. It is a matter of taste, pure and simple. Also some common sense. For example, I would certainly want a comparatively dainty letter for a poster calculated to appeal to a feminine audience. For a poster advertising tractors, on the other hand, I naturally would be inclined to employ a lettering style that is bold and vigorous and suggests the behemoth proportions of the product. Where the Eve, the Huxley, or fine scripts would be appropriate, the Neuland, Beton, or heavy Gothics would be out of tune.

Q. What is your favorite poster alphabet?

A. At present, it is a condensed Gothic style which artists have nicknamed Gaspipe. Printers call it Franklin Gothic Condensed. I said "at present" because taste in lettering, as in everything else, changes with the times. It seems that the so-called Gaspipe alphabet is the current favorite of many poster artists. At a recent Art Directors' Club exhibit, seven posters out of ten were lettered with a modified version of this alphabet. I can recall when such popularity was held by the informal Cooper style.

Q. Is the Gaspipe a difficult letter to master?

A. No. And that may explain why it is so popular. It is an easy letter to construct and fairly simple to space correctly.

Q. What do you do, make up your own styles or copy from existing styles?

A. Both. During the course of my professional experience, I have developed many styles which are more or less personalized versions of current favorites. I also refer frequently to the latest typefaces and copy them outright, or change them in some way to suit my purpose.

Q. Is there any law, we mean a copyright restriction, against copying a standard typeface and using it on a poster without permission from the type foundry?

A. There is no legal restriction against copying any typeface. As long as you don't set yourself up in business to cast duplicates of existing typefaces, it's all right with the constable.

Q. You have not made it clear yet whether the average artist ever designs original alphabets.

A. Few poster artists will sit down to design an alphabet. That is the business of typographers and type designers. Most letterers gradually evolve a few styles so distinctly personal that they virtually constitute original designs. Personally, I hesitate to depart too far from current styles. The more radical the departure from usage, the less legible an alphabet generally becomes.

Q. How does one go about doing the lettering on a poster?

A. Everyone has his own system and varies the procedure to fit his purpose. There is no fixed rule. Here's how I go about it. If the poster I am working on represents an important commission and will be reproduced in great quantities, I naturally take more time with it. For such a job, I usually follow this procedure:

On a separate sheet of cardboard I lay out the guide lines for the lettering and sketch in the copy freehand, in pencil. In this first draft I am more concerned with getting character and even-toned spacing than precision. From this I trace the lettering onto a piece of transparent paper, making corrections in spacing and letter construction as I go along. Then I smudge the back of this tracing paper with chalk or charcoal, depending upon whether the painted background of my poster is dark or light. I fasten the smudged tracing in position on the poster, and go over the lettering with a fairly hard pencil.

Q. Is the lettering now ready to be painted in?

A. Not yet. That is, not on those special jobs that I just mentioned. Traced guide lines always come out smudgy, irregular, and variable in thickness. The work is not sharp enough to be followed with exactness. To correct this, I lightly rub art gum or a chamois cloth over all the traced lines, leaving only a faint impression of the forms of the letters. Now I go over this faint impression carefully with a well-sharpened pencil. This, by the way, gives me still another chance to make changes before painting in.

Q. What tools do you use for painting in your lettering?

A. That depends on the type of letter. For a trim-looking Gaspipe most artists like to outline the vertical and horizontal strokes with a ruling pen, paint in the elbow curves with a small brush, and then fill it all in with a larger brush. Personally, I prefer to take my chances doing the entire letter with a lettering brush, freehand. The lines may not be as sharp that way, but what my lettering lacks in mechanical precision, it more than makes up for in character. Of course, for certain styles like the Neuland, Weiss, Legend, and the Cursive Scripts, the ruling pen cannot be used even by those who are addicted to it; it must all be brush work.

Q. What about jobs where the lettering does not have to be too "finished?" We refer to lettering for a temporary poster or show card.

A. For such work I follow a different procedure. I pencil in light guide lines directly on the poster, quickly ghost-sketch the copy, and without further ado, brush in the lettering with paint. Such a direct approach, it goes without saying, calls for dexterity in handling the show card brush, a sense of spacing, and an intimate knowledge of letter formation.

Q. What advice would you give to one who is interested in learning the kind of fine lettering used on posters and in magazine advertisements?

A. To state it briefly, learn the freehand brush technique before taking up reproduction lettering. With such a background, you will find that lettering need not be mechanical drudgery; it can be as delightful an experience as any creative art endeavor.

CHAPTER FOUR

THE MYSTERY OF COLOR

WHAT is a millimicron? Nine out of ten artists would be stumped. The average physicist, however, will have a ready answer. A millimicron is a billionth part of a meter. It is a unit of measure used to designate the wave lengths of the various spectrum colors comprising white light.

What is the Ladd-Franklin theory? The Duplicating theory? The Eldridge-Green theory?

Artists work and thrive in blissful ignorance of these and other scientific theories. Color to artists is largely a matter of intuition and taste.

It is an exasperating and often fruitless undertaking for the artist interested in poster-making to venture too deeply into the mystery of color. An enormous amount of data on the subject has been compiled, part of which is verified by scientific experiment, part still hardly more than conjecture, all of which is of greater significance to the specialized interests of color physicists and paint chemists than to the average poster artist. There are artists who have run away with the honors time and again who do not profess to know half as much about the science of color as do chemists and laboratory workers who may never have held a paint brush in their hands. These artists are like big-league ball players who have an inherent aptitude for the game, without knowing the natural laws pertaining to velocity and inertia, or the scientific principles pertaining to a body in motion.

Without entering too studiously into a scientific study of color, let us review the generally accepted theory which maintains that white light is the synthesis of all colors. This phenomenon was first noted by Sir Isaac Newton in 1666. It was his conviction that all colors are present in sunlight. He proved it by directing a beam of sunlight on a diamond-shaped glass prism. It is an experiment with which we are by now all familiar. The prism acts as a sort of screen and breaks up the apparently white light into an imperceptible gradation of colors. This array of colors Newton called the Spectrum. He arbitrarily divided this spectrum into seven broad regions and designated them as violet, indigo, blue, green, yellow, orange and red. The spectrum colors can be re-combined to form white light. The rainbow is the best natural example of the phenomenon of the dispersion of light; the raindrops suspended in the air act as miniature prisms and break up the white light of the sun into the elemental colors.

The different color sensations, scientists point out, are due to the difference in wave lengths of the various colors. They go on to explain that light waves travel as electromagnetic impulses. The human eye can perceive only a small portion of the entire spectrum because the human field of vision is limited to wave lengths ranging from four hundred billionths to seven hundred billionths of a meter. It is such astronomical infinitesmals that frighten the poor commercial artist away from a scientific investigation of color.

Just how we perceive color is not yet incontestably established. The Young-Helmholtz theory holds that red, green and blue-violet are the primaries which form the nucleus for all other colors. The human eye is equipped with three sets of special color nerves, each of which is responsive to one of these three primaries. If the three color nerves are acted upon simultaneously, the resulting color sensation is white.

There are theories to challenge this one. The Brewster theory for example, contends that blue, red and yellow are the true primaries. This is disputed by physicists, but oddly enough it is the one theory that seems acceptable to artists and printers. All paint mixing and multicolor reproduction work is based on this selection of primaries. But we have had enough. As far as the practicing artist is concerned, aside from satisfying a purely cultural curiosity, there is little in most of these theories to help him directly in the choice or use of colors for his next poster. Let us forsake scientific speculation for less lofty though more practical considerations.

Most of us react pretty much the same way to color stimuli. Our response to color is conditioned by traditional association of colors with things about us. To most people, for instance, white suggests purity and cleanliness. Black, though traditionally a mourning color, imparts a feeling of elegance and formality. Violet calls to mind tender and pious associations. Purple is the color of royalty and authority. When combined with black and green, purple also hints at intrigue and mystery. Red is the symbol of revolution, excitement, fire and fury. Blue has always been the color of sadness and night. Traditionally associated with subjects relating to the sea, blue also suggests coldness and quietude. Yellow is a warm color producing a glowing atmosphere of optimism, summer sunshine, and light. Green is suggestive of things pertaining to spring and vernal growth. Pink is definitely a feminine color, expressing delicacy and daintiness. Practically every color has some such symbolic association.

Generally speaking, colors may be divided as advancing colors and receding colors. The receding colors such as greens, blues, and violets give the feeling of coolness and tranquility; while the advancing colors such as yellow, orange, and red psychologically suggest warmth and excitement. Offhand, one would be inclined to say that if a poster is to compel attention, it should be painted in advancing colors. However, we must realize that it is not isolated colors that matter; it is the combination of colors that contributes to the attraction value of a poster. For example, yellow (an advancing color) if applied on a white card is hardly discernible. Yet that same yellow, placed against black, makes a powerful combination.

Legibility is a matter of contrast. Attempts have been made to list color combinations in the order of their contrast value. Such legibility scales are not too scientific, as they do not specify the particular value or chroma of the respective colors, the relative area covered by each, nor the nature of the lighting under which the colors will be viewed. All these factors are important. Since the following is the most widely accepted scale, it is presented here for what it is worth:

1. Black on a yellow background
2. Black on a white "
3. Yellow on a black "
4. White on a black "
5. Blue on a white "
6. White on a blue "
7. White on a green "
8. Green on a white background
9. Red on a white "
10. White on a red "
11. Black on an orange "
12. Orange on a black "
13. Red on a green "
14. Green on a red "

MUNSELL COLOR NOTATION

There has long been a need for some sort of system to identify each color by an objective symbol rather than by purely personal and often whimsical attempts at literal descriptions. Popular color terminology includes the names of flowers, vegetables, minerals, geographic locations, and so forth. To contribute to the confusion, manufacturers of cosmetics and specialties have dreamed up dawn gray, baby pink, mist green, shocking red, and other such fanciful names which have become part of the bedeviled dictionary of color notation.

To Professor A. H. Munsell goes the credit not only for calling attention to the inadequacy of arbitrary color names, but for doing something constructive about it. In 1899, after lengthy research, Munsell devised a workable system of color notation which has since been accepted by the Bureau of Standards in Washington, D. C. The Munsell System designates a graphic symbol for each existing color in terms of its hue, value, and chroma—and is flexible enough to allow for classification by symbol of any possible color ever to be developed.

Munsell based his analysis of color on the premise that color can be viewed from three different aspects. He pointed out that just as a box has three dimensions—length, width, and breadth—so color can be said to possess three dimensions—hue, value, and chroma. *Hue* is the nature of a color which makes us distinguish one from another. It is the quality by which we differentiate red from yellow or blue or any other color. *Value* is the quality of a color which denotes its lightness or darkness. We say one thing is light blue, and another is dark blue. *Chroma* is the purity of a color. The stronger the color, the greater its purity. A color that looks grayish is weak in chroma. A color that has a high degree of distinguishable purity is said to be high in chroma. To illustrate, in describing a color as a "bright light green," the word *bright* refers to the chroma, *light* designates the value, and *green* stands for the particular hue.

First, Munsell arranged his colors in a hue circuit divided into ten principal sections, and designated the hues as red, yellow-red, yellow, green-yellow, green, blue-green, blue, purple-blue, purple, red-purple. The range of light and dark values he illustrated graphically by a vertical pole with scaled-off divisions representing nine progressive shades of gray between black and white. Black was placed just under the pole, each of the nine divisions marked an increasingly lighter gray from one to nine, and white was just above the pole. A very dark color, for example a deep maroon, might be #2 on such a scale of values. To refer to it numerically as Munsell might, we would designate this shade of maroon as R/2; the letter R standing for the hue (red) and the numeral 2 for the value (dark). Munsell indicated the chroma scale on a horizontal band running square to the value axis, where, as the color approximates gray, it is closer to the axis and as it becomes brighter, it is further removed. The notation R2/2 would designate a red, dark in value, close to gray in chroma. R3/8 would show that the color is dark red, but quite strong in chroma. R8/3 would indicate a light red or pink.

The Munsell System, which makes it possible to designate graphically any existing or conceivable color through the use of logical symbols, is more elaborate than our explanation indicates. What has been said here merely suggests the idea behind the system. This color code has not as yet been adopted by many artists, though it is used by a number of paint and ink manufacturers and by large printing establishments.

COLOR HARMONY

Color is the lifeblood of a poster. But it is not how many colors are used on a poster design, but what the colors are and how well they are related that is important. A design in fifteen colors is not necessarily more impressive than one confined to three or four. As a matter of fact, if too many colors are used, the allover effect is bound to be a discordant hodgepodge. Not only does the extravagant use of color destroy the potency of a poster, but it may also create technical and financial problems in getting the job printed. A poster designed in a few colors and laid out in simple areas will be welcomed by any printing house.

To the enterprising artist, restrictions regarding the number of colors he may use is a challenge, not a hindrance. He knows that each color must be put to work, and that all colors must work in unison to insure a harmonious composition. The laws relating to color harmony have been classified as follows:

Monochromatic Harmony. Harmony attained in a color scheme where different values of the same hue are used. Light brown, medium brown and dark brown, or other such gradations of one color make for a conservative color scheme. Conservative but not compelling.

Related or Analogous Harmony. Harmony attained in a color scheme based on the use of hues that are adjacent on the color wheel and are of the same primary family. Yellow, yellow-red, and red show a pleasing kinship. So do blue, blue-green, and green, and also other combinations of colors which are close to each other on the color wheel.

Complementary Harmony. Harmony attained in a color scheme based on the use of hues that are directly opposite each other on the color wheel, such as orange and blue, red and green, and so forth. However, an unpleasant optical vibration results if each of the complementaries is of the same value and chroma.

Triad Harmony. Harmony attained in a color scheme by the use of any three colors so located on the color wheel that they form the points of an imaginary equilateral triangle. No matter which way the triangle is turned, the colors at the three points will be in harmony. Example: green, yellow-red, and purple-blue.

Split-Complementary Harmony. Harmony attained in a color scheme by the use of a given color with the two colors situated on either side of its complementary. Example: yellow with red-purple and purple-blue.

Double-Complementary Harmony. Harmony attained in a color scheme through the use of two sets of complementary colors on the one design. Red, green, yellow, and purple are a popular color combination.

It is comparatively easy to get a harmonious color combination. The course of least resistance would be to use a monochromatic color scheme. Though this is a safe procedure and invariably produces a harmonious relationship between colors, it is not spectacular nor exciting. If one seeks excitement in a color scheme, it can be accomplished easily through the use of complementary colors of high chroma and equal value. But this sort of excitement is often irritating, and does not leave the beholder with a sense of satisfaction. How can these apparent differences be reconciled? How can the contrasting colors of a poster be made forceful enough to compel attention yet produce a feeling of harmony?

There are several ways to avert a color clash and to stabilize the optical tension of two complementary colors. A third color may be introduced to maintain the balance. A black or white outline painted around each color area will serve as a fence to keep the opposing colors from getting at each other. Another way to get this "harmony of contrasts" is to make adjustments in the value and chroma strength of the complementaries to give prominence to one color at the expense of another.

Just as it is known that two complementary colors intensify one another when placed side by side, all colors are known to be affected to some degree by their surroundings. Several laws have been formulated relating to the effect that colors have upon each other.

Law of Simultaneous Contrast of Value. When a dark color is placed beside a light color, the dark color will appear darker and the light color lighter. A strip of gray on a black background apparently becomes lighter in value and makes the black appear deeper.

Law of Simultaneous Contrast of Chroma. When a dull color or one weak in chroma is placed next to a color strong in chroma, the dull color will appear duller and the strong color will take on a greater brilliance. When a strip of grayish green is placed on a bright green background, the strip seems to get grayer while the background seems more vivid by contrast.

Law of Simultaneous Contrast of Hue. Colors placed next to each other appear to be tinged with their complementaries. A strip of blue on a red background will take on a greenish cast, green being the complementary of red. The red will take on an orange cast, since orange is the complement of blue.

When all is said and done, color taste remains something aesthetic and personal. While a familiarity with the laws of color harmony and contrast is helpful, there are so many factors that enter into the selection of colors for a poster design, that each rule is qualified by too many exceptions to be followed implicitly.

THE CHEMISTRY OF PAINT

The ancient masters were more versed in the chemistry of paint than are modern commercial artists. They had to be. In the first place, they were seriously concerned about the permanence of their work; it was their aim to produce masterpieces that would endure. Then too, it was imperative for them to learn about the nature of pigments and oils for they had to prepare their own working materials. Although the modern commercial artist is not driven by necessity to make his own colors, it might be of academic interest to him to know something about the make-up of paint. The most important ingredients in paint are pigments, vehicles, and binders.

Pigments. There are two kinds of pigments: active and inert. Active pigments are finely ground particles of earth, mineral, vegetable or animal matter, which impart their natural color to the liquid with which they are mixed. Inert pigments are substances without color potency. They are used to "dope up" or extend the volume of paint.

Vehicles. The vehicle is the fluid used to carry the pigment particles so that the paint will spread evenly. The determining difference between one type of paint and another is not in the pigment, but in the vehicle with which the pigment is intermixed. In poster colors the vehicle is water; in oil paints it is oil or varnish; in dyes the vehicle is water or alcohol.

Binding Agents. The binding agent in poster color is mucilage, gum arabic, or other such substance, which is intermixed with the pigment and vehicle. While the purpose of the vehicle is to float the pigment particles, it is the function of the binder to anchor the particles so that they will adhere to the surface upon which they are applied. Paint that is deficient in this ingredient will rub off, as there is not enough binder to make the pigment cling after the water or other vehicle has evaporated.

The type of paint used in poster work is an opaque tempera preparation commercially known as show card color or poster color. The finer grade of tempera color, though not a strict requisite for poster work, is preferred by some artists, and is sold in tubes only. For all practical poster purposes, any good show card color sold in jars is satisfactory. In a good grade of paint, the color is pure, strong, and opaque. It is free from grit and brushes well. Inferior colors are doped up (for obvious commercial reasons) with lots of inert pigment. They have an undesirable granular texture, they fade more rapidly than pure colors, dry with a chalky effect, and have a tendency to crack after a period of time.

The best poster and tempera colors were formerly imported from Germany and England, but today our domestic brands compare favorably with the foreign products. Some say that our colors have now been developed beyond the standards of high quality set forth by European manufacturers. In view of the availability of good poster colors at reasonable prices, it would be perverted economy for the commercial artist to devote valuable time and effort in the home preparation of paints.

Q. Perhaps you can tell us why there is such confusion and conflict in color theories?

A. The root of the confusion lies in the fact that the theories that apply to color in *light* do not apply to color in *pigments*. As you know, the three paint primaries are red, yellow, and blue. They are subtractive in nature. This means that a dab of paint on white paper, no matter how transparent the paint may be, blocks out some of the color rays reflected by the white surface, so that only a partial spectrum filters through. You have probably seen catalogues of ink manufacturers where three circles—one red, one yellow, and one blue—are printed so that they overlap each other partially. The area where all three overlap appears black, because no light rays filter through from the original white. Each of the primaries subtracts its share from the total spectrum of light.

The light primaries are not the same in either identity or behavior as the pigment primaries. The primary colors in light are red, green, and blue, and they are additive in nature. When three spotlights—one red, one green, and one blue—are focused to converge, they add up to form white—white being the sum total of the three light primaries.

CHAPTER FOUR

Q. What are achromatic colors?

A. Black, white, and all the intermediate shades of gray are known as achromatic colors. According to the dictionary, the term means "colorless colors." According to the Munsell Notation, these colors just have value but no chroma.

Q. According to this explanation, black and white are not really colors. We'd like to believe that but find it difficult. Why are black and white, pigments that are so indispensable to every artist, not ranked as colors?

A. Scientifically speaking, white is the presence of all colors and black is the absence of all colors. White objects reflect all light rays and black objects absorb all light and reflect none. This distinction, however interesting, is purely academic as far as the artist is concerned. To him black and white are positive effects, and hold an important place on his palette, whether science acknowledges it or not. A scientifically minded friend of mine explained to me some time ago that when we look at black lettering on white paper, we are not actually aware of the presence of lettering; what we do see, is the absence of light in restricted shapes.

Q. Thank you for passing on this confusion. Let's turn to more practical considerations. Would you say that a palette of red, yellow, and blue, plus black and white are sufficient for obtaining all other colors through intermixing?

A. No. It would not be possible to get all colors this way. Yellow and blue, for example, will give you green, but to get a particular shade of green you must mix a certain blue with a certain yellow. I personally have an assortment of more than a dozen distinct key colors. To get a bright emerald green by intermixing, I use lemon yellow and turquoise blue. For a chrome green, I mix chrome yellow with bulletin blue. To get a vivid purple, I mix cerise red with cerulean blue, and so on.

Q. We know that gray can be made by mixing white and black, yet we have been unable to mix a gray that is not streaky. How do you do it?

A. I buy the gray ready-mixed. Theoretically, gray is produced by the admixture of white and black but tempera colors so mixed seldom dry free from traces of the two ingredients. It is better to include in your stock at least one jar of neutral gray, from which you can derive lighter and darker shades.

Which reminds me of a funny experience I once had—only it didn't seem funny at the time. When I was an apprentice in a large printing establishment where posters were reproduced in quantity, my first assignment was to help in the paint department. One day I was given an empty five-gallon paint can and told to match up a three-gallon mixture of a light gray. I began with two and one-half gallons of black, and daintily added a little white. As there was no visible change in the color, I cautiously added some more white. By this time there was already more than three gallons of paint but not even faintly resembling gray. I now added a generous portion of white and was rewarded by a slight change. The black lost its intensity but was still a far cry from the color I had to match. A bit panicky at this stage of the game, I opened a fresh gallon can of white and dumped in the entire contents. The more than four-gallon mixture was still depressingly dark—shades deeper than the color swatch that was pinned up for me to duplicate.

A thought occurred to me. Perhaps I had started with the wrong color. It might have been better to have started with white and added black. But it was too late to begin all over again. In fact, it was impossible, for I ran short of white paint. As the five-gallon can was now full, I poured off part of my gray mixture into some of the empty cans lately relieved of their contents of virgin white. I tucked away these samples of indeterminate gray in hidden corners of the studio, and poured my last gallon of white into the big can. At last there appeared a gray remotely resembling the color swatch. Very guiltily and with suppressed anxiety, I presented three gallons of gray to the production man and got his OK on it. I breathed a sigh of relief when that ordeal was over and was about to thank the Lord, when the man in charge of another department asked me to bring him a few gallons of white. But what happened then is another story.

Q. Do you believe in making your own paints?

A. Decidedly not. I am a poster artist, not a paint chemist. I do not make my own brushes, I do not make my own cardboard, I do not make my own pencils. We live in a commercial world and a competent artist need not be a Robinson Crusoe.

I remember an interesting afternoon I spent in the laboratories of a paint company observing how pigments are ground and mixed and how vehicles are formulated. What I saw was enough to convince me that the making of paints is a science in itself. What is more, it requires facilities that I could never hope to duplicate in my own studio. I get my paints ready-made, just as other commercial artists do.

Q. We notice that you match your paints under artificial light. It has been our impression that it is better to match colors in direct sunlight or at least in daylight.

A. It is. That is, daylight is good, but direct sunlight is not. Sunlight produces a disturbing glare due to strong surface reflection. The reason I happen to be matching my colors in artificial light now is that the poster on which I am at work will, when printed, be posted in the subway stations where it will be seen under artificial light.

Q. We notice too that you try out your color and allow it to dry before using it on your poster. Is there a good reason for this procedure?

A. Yes, there certainly is. As paint dries, its color undergoes a slight change. Most paints appear duller and lighter when dry, but there is no way of knowing what effect drying will have on a color unless you actually try it out.

Q. Just what is the difference between a tint and a shade?

A. A tint is a mixture of a color with white, to increase its value; a shade is a mixture of a color with black, to lower its value.

Q. Gold and silver are not seen much on posters, nor are they mentioned as colors. Why is that?

A. These metallic paints are not mentioned as colors because they are not part of the spectrum. Nor are they popular with poster artists. They are gaudy and they cannot be intermixed with one another or with any spectrum color. What is more, metallic paints have a tendency to tarnish after exposure. Printers will thank you if you refrain from using gold and silver, as they entail technical difficulties in printing.

Q. It is said that when using a combination of a powerful color with one that is subdued, it is best to confine the more aggressive color to a small area of focal interest. Is that true?

A. Not necessarily. I have seen some excellent posters where orange-red (the most advancing of colors) was used for the greatest area, the background. It is true, though, that on a neutral or subdued background, a color of strong chroma is definitely an eye-catcher, even if it occupies but a small spot on the poster.

Q. In judging a shade or matching it to another color, how do you manage to isolate it so you can see it without being visually distracted by the colors surrounding it?

A. I cut a small rectangular window in a large piece of opaque paper and place it over the color to be matched. If two colors are to be compared, two masks are used. This isolates each color from its surroundings and eliminates the optical effect that adjacent colors have on each other.

Q. We have seen some wonderful ads showing an inexpensive mechanical device for getting thousands of color combinations automatically. All you do, the ads say, is rotate a disc and presto, you have at your fingertips the color combination that suits your purpose! What do you think of this automatic color selector?

A. It is more ingenious than practical. No doubt it can be a valuable guide for art students, for amateur textile designers and interior decorators. But professional artists do not rely on it.

Q. How do you explain that?

A. The use of the color selector is limited because it cannot show the all-over effect resulting from the combination of varying color areas. It is no guide for the balance of color, for legibility, or for appropriateness of color to subject. To a real artist, color selection involves more than spinning a wheel. Color is a matter of taste and discretion, and these elusive ingredients cannot be doled out by any mechanical device or mathematical formula. Just as a poet cannot turn for his inspiration to a rhyming dictionary, so an artist cannot hope to settle the choice of his color scheme by spinning a color disc.

CHAPTER FIVE

YOU DEVELOP A STYLE

THE work of outstanding commercial artists is easily recognizable, due to the individualized technique they use to present the subject matter. This stamp of individuality by which an artist's work can be identified is commonly referred to as his style or his technique. The dissimilarity between a Howard Scott poster and an Otis Shepard poster is marked. Each artist approaches the problem in his own manner.

In general, poster styles fall into two categories: one emphasizes realism and the other emphasizes design. Which of these treatments makes for a better poster is a controversial subject among artists in America. The prevalence of realism and naturalism, and the comparative absence of symbolic design on our billboards and window displays, indicate pretty conclusively the relative influence exerted by each of these opposing schools of art. Let us review the case for each side.

THE REALISTIC SCHOOL

"Give the people what they like." That philosophic colloquialism sums up the attitude of artists who subscribe to the realistic school of poster art. It is not necessarily an expression of what they themselves like, but what they feel the public and the advertisers want. Many an exponent of realism will confide that as far as his own taste goes, he personally prefers posters that are more than mere story-telling illustrations. But since it is to the public that the advertiser appeals through the medium of the poster, it is no more than right that poster art should reflect public taste. To strike a responsive cord with the masses, it has been found that posters must show pictures of real people and real scenes. The illustrations must be delineated with photographic fidelity and even exaggerated here and there to make a situation clearer than it is possible to do with a camera.

The chasm between photographic art and realistic drawing is narrowing, so that in many cases one medium can be substituted for the other. Photography has already invaded and usurped a large part of the poster-artist's domain. Constant improvement in color photography has extended its use for poster illustration. Don't get the impression from this that there is any warfare going on between photographers and illustrators. Not at all. Whatever professional resentment the artist originally showed to the intruding camera has by now been long forgotten. As a matter of fact, the progressive commercial artist has adopted the camera and has learned how best to apply it to his own needs. Mention of the camera is made here not so much to show its technical service to the artist, but rather to indicate how strong is the public's demand for photographic realism in poster art. Whether by photograph or drawing—the wistful baby crying for a certain cereal, the perspiring policeman refreshing himself with a popular soft drink, the pretty girl happy in the possession of that automatic toaster, the contented painter wearing a hat upon which is inscribed with remarkable clarity the brand name of the advertiser's paint—all are depicted with convincing realism. The artist makes sure to leave nothing to the imagination.

A renowned critic of American poster art, in talking about the hypernaturalism that is demanded of the poster artist, mentioned the incident of an art director who, in discussing a painting of a typical freckled country lad, told the artist that the client liked the illustration but thought that there were not quite enough freckles. Americans have a sweet tooth for Pollyanna sentimentality and have always responded favorably to simple stories and humor. Those posters which require the least amount of mental exertion for comprehension appeal to them most. This deeply rooted national characteristic accounts for the unceasing popularity of the radio soap operas, movies, romantic novels, and picture magazines. "As long as this is the type of advertising that interests the American people, by all means let's give it to them," seems to be the motto of the realistic school.

THE CREATIVE DESIGN SCHOOL

The credo of the poster artists who subscribe to the school of creative design may be summed up in the following observations:

1. Poster art need not cater to public taste. If possible, it should help to educate and elevate the general level of taste.
2. A poster should appeal to the intellect, not to shallow sentimentality.
3. A poster should make an impression, not tell a story.

4. A poster should be presented in a form startlingly different from the natural, so that the random gaze of the passer-by will be attracted and riveted to it.

Conclusively stated, a symbolic design can better fulfill the aims of a poster than drawings and illustrations presented with commonplace realism.

PAINTING TECHNIQUES

As we said in the opening paragraph of this chapter, every artist has his own distinct style and manner of painting. For posters treated with illustrative realism, the painting techniques are identical with those used by fine artists and illustrators. Since the general art of painting and illustrating is too broad a subject to be taken up here, and has been aptly covered in numerous books, we shall concentrate only on those techniques which lend themselves especially to the type of poster based on creative design. Along with the procedure for each technique, the important tools and materials will be listed.

FLAT TONE TECHNIQUE

That painting in flat tones is not so simple as it seems, is evidenced by the struggle that beginners encounter in this phase of the painting of a poster. To get an even coat of paint over a large area, say for the background of a poster, you must start with the right kind of cardboard, the proper brush, and the most suitable paint for the purpose.

The Board. It is easier to get a flat coat of paint on a dull and slightly grained cardboard than on a smooth board. Paint does not absorb evenly on glossy stock and usually dries with streaky effects. Wattman Illustration Board, an imported brand, possesses just the right surface finish and texture. It is available in sizes 22 inches by 30 inches, 27 inches by 40 inches, and 30 inches by 52 inches. Domestic illustration board, a good substitute for Wattman's, comes in sheets 40 inches by 60 inches.

The thickness of the cardboard is an important factor, too. As paint dries, it shrinks the surface upon which it is applied. This shrinkage in turn, leads to buckling or wrinkling and is more pronounced on thin paper than on heavy stock. For best results, it is advisable to get a good grade of substantial illustration board. Colored poster boards, known as show card stock, can be had in more than thirty different colors as well as in gold and silver, but in spite of this assortment of colors, most artists prefer to paint in their own backgrounds. Show card board does not have so rich a texture as illustration board and is used more for temporary posters and show cards than for designs intended for reproduction.

The Painting Mediums. There are three types of coloring mediums that may be used for poster work: tube tempera colors, jar show card colors, and inks. The most popular of the three is the species of tempera color put up in jars and sold as show card paint. One art dealer lists about fifty different colors and shades in his catalogue, but few artists find a need for the entire assortment. White, black, spectrum gray, Prussian blue, turquoise blue, lemon yellow, chrome yellow, vermillion, magenta, brilliant orange, and perhaps one or two others, should form enough of a nucleus for most practical purposes.

The better quality show card paints have good opacity, are of a smooth creamy consistency, and dry with a flat finish. For more brilliant effects, tube paints are recommended. Although they are finely ground in the process of manufacture and are very smooth to work with, not all poster artists like them. The jar colors, being of a fluid consistency, need only the addition of a little water and they are all ready to apply. Tube colors on the other hand, being of a paste consistency, require a little more mixing and diluting before they are ready for use.

Inks are not so popular with poster artists as paints. In the first place, although they come in many different colors, all the colors with the exception of black are transparent. Then too, inks are watery and not quite so manageable where flat tones are required. Those artists who have learned to work with inks praise them for their brilliant iridescent quality.

The Brushes. The best type of brushes to use for general poster work are the same as those used for show card lettering. While they can be used for any poster painting technique, they are especially suitable when smooth flat tones are wanted. A flat-ferruled "fill in" or "single stroke" brush will expedite the job of filling in large areas. These brushes are classified according to linear inch, their natural chisel measuring from 1/8 of an inch to 1 inch.

To paint in a large area so that it will dry with a flat uniform finish, free from streaks, be sure first of all to mix a sufficient quantity of paint and then check to see that it is of the proper working consistency. That is very important. Poster color that is properly mixed flows freely and will not cause the brush to drag along as it is stroked. Use the widest chisel-edged brush in your collection, and stroke the paint in long parallel lines, making the strokes overlap each other slightly. To be sure that the area has been thoroughly covered, and at the same time, to distribute the paint more evenly, turn the card and pass the brush over the area again, using very little additional paint. This time make parallel strokes that run perpendicular to the original brush strokes. Take care to brush out the paint evenly so that none will accumulate in puddles on the board. Should you find that the paint has become too thick to work with, don't dip your brush into a water jar after each helping of paint, hoping by this means to thin it. It is better to stop and thin down the entire batch of color. To prevent the paint from thickening, keep your mixed color in a jar, glass, or dish, not on a piece of cardboard. An absorbent surface tends to suck in the water of the paint, and as a consequence, the paint gets thicker by degrees.

While the card is drying, it should not be stood up on end, leaned against any object, nor placed so that it extends beyond the edge of the table. If the painted card does not lie flat while it dries, it will become so warped that it will be almost impossible to get it straight again. These precautions, while intended primarily for painting large areas, are to a degree applicable to the painting of any area of a poster where a flat even tone is required.

SIMPLIFIED SILHOUETTE TECHNIQUE

We are all familiar with the well-designed symbolic figures representing the farmer, the college professor, the busy factory, the schoolhouse, and other equally delightful pictograph designs which are to be found on statistical charts and tables. On a grander scale, the same conventionalized forms can be the basis for pictorial designs on posters. The artist who treats his subject in this symbolic manner makes no attempt whatever to give the illusion of modeling. He limits his drawing to the simplest shapes and the barest essentials, striving for a flat, two-dimensional design, not a lifelike illustration. The figures are mere silhouettes, simplified along geometric lines and calling for an economy of line and color.

One of the best ways to render a subject in terms of these simplified shapes is to follow a procedure something like this:

1. Study the subject you want to portray, searching for distinctive and strongly identifiable features that can be represented in simple shapes.
2. Design a simple silhouette figure composed of shapes that incorporate the outstanding characteristics of the subject.
3. Draw each of these component elements of the design on a separate piece of colored paper.
4. Cut out these colored shapes and fit them together as a composition on a card the same color as you plan for the background of the poster. When cutting out the shapes, it is a good idea to cut through several different-colored sheets at the same time. This will give you each shape in a variety of colors.
5. Experiment by moving the shapes around, trying out the effects of different colors and different shapes. Alternate shapes may be cut

out for any element of the design, to allow for experimentation with new combinations.

6. When a satisfactory color and shape combination is arrived at, paste the pieces down on the card.
7. Copy or trace this composition onto the poster board and paint in the areas, using the paste-up *collage* as a guide.

FLAT PATCH TECHNIQUE

The flat color painting technique need not be confined to the stark simplicity of silhouette-like treatment. With the proper division of area and a good play of color, flat colors can be made to give the visual impression of three-dimensional modeling. The flat patch technique is very popular for movie posters which are designed around portraits of the actors or dramatic scenes from the motion pictures. Naturally this technique has wider scope. It can be used for practically any commercial poster where a realistic yet striking effect is desired.

In essence, the treatment resolves itself to this. The subject matter is presented in a limited number of colors, each of which is kept in a distinct boundary. In order to get a breakup of color, it is treated as if seen under powerful lights, with contrasting divisions of strong highlights and deep shadows. This play of light and dark brings out strong characteristics and does away with minor variations in tone. Blending of tones is purely optical. Actually the artist uses flat colors in patches or geometric shapes. This results in a picture which is really a patchwork or mosaic of distinct colors so fitted together as to give shape and a semblance of modeling to the subject. This technique is a cross between the stark simplicity of a silhouette and the photographic authenticity of a camera study. At one of the large New York studios, which makes a specialty of movie posters treated in this style, the artists recommend the following procedure which they have found practical.

1. Obtain a photograph of the subject you wish to portray. The type of commercial "glossy" used for movie stills is ideal. The photographic print should be sharp and clear with strong highlights and deep shadows.
2. Copy or trace onto illustration board, all the structural lines as well as the definite shadow and highlight boundaries that appear on the photograph. In work where the illustration is to appear larger than the available "glossy," the photo can be enlarged to the required size by means of a standard projection machine. A key tracing made of the projected image serves as the groundwork for the painted picture. In

this manner much time is saved and greater accuracy is assured.

3. Decide how many colors you are going to use and what they are to be. It is always economical to limit the number of colors—five or six are ample for most commercial posters of this kind. The light and dark values on the photograph serve as a guide for the ultimate choice of colors. The darkest areas on the photo are interpreted in terms of low-value colors on the painting. The same relationship holds good for other values.
4. Make a key color swatch of the colors you are going to use and label each one with a numeral or a letter. On the tracing, indicate within each distinct color area the appropriate symbol corresponding to the color swatch. For instance, light brown, which may be number 4 on your color key, may appear in the drawing as a shadow under the nose, as a small area under the eyes, and a goodly portion of the side of the face. You would, therefore, lightly pencil in a small figure 4 in each of these areas to guide you in painting.
5. Paint in the marked areas on the illustration board, using colors corresponding to the code on the sample color swatch.

AIRBRUSH TECHNIQUE

Whereas artists' bristle brushes have been used for hundreds of years, the airbrush is, historically speaking, a new tool. Patented in 1890, the airbrush was originally employed as a device for touching up photographs and adding surface texture to architectural and industrial drawings. As artists began to experiment with this new device, they realized that it offered a novel painting style impossible to attain with any other tool.

Fundamentally, the operational principle of the airbrush does not differ much from that of the insecticide spray gun or the familiar seltzer bottle. A spray is ejected through a nozzle by the force of compressed air.

Airbrush Unit. The airbrush unit consists of the brush or "pencil," as it is sometimes called, and the air compressor. There are several kinds of compressors. One kind is the torpedo-shaped metal tank which contains compressed carbonic gas. This is really not a compressor in the sense that it compresses air; it is a storage tank which holds air previously forced into it. A flexible rubber hose is coupled to an escape valve on top of the tank, where a gauge registers the amount of air that flows through the hose and into the brush. The tank is not purchased outright; it is serviced on a rental basis. As one tank is emptied, it is replaced by a new one. The advantages this has over other types of air supply is that it is noiseless and the air can be released in a steady flow. Its main limitation is that it has to be recharged at intervals.

In the electrically operated type of compressor, air pressure is created by a motor-driven pump. Air is manufactured as it is needed. When the motor is shut off, the flow of air ceases immediately. This type of compressor is quite noisy. During the time that the pumping operation is going on, there is a steady chug-chug sound, faintly reminiscent of an outboard motor. This pumping action also causes a slight pulsation in the flow of air, resulting in a spray which is not as constant as that of the stored-air compressor. This entire unit is portable, being equipped with either a grip handle or coasters, so that it may be carried or rolled to wherever it is needed.

The third type of compressor is an electric unit fitted out with a metal tank for storing air compressed by the action of its pump. When the tank is filled to capacity, the motor automatically shuts itself off, to resume its work only when pressure runs low. With this machine, there is no pulsation in the spray, since the air that reaches the brush is stored air, coming from the tank reservoir, not from the direct action of the pump. The noise is also cut down considerably since the motor operates only during alternate periods, when the stock of air runs low. Regardless of the built-up pressure stored in the tank, the artist can control the force with which the air is released.

The airbrush instrument, though only the size of an overgrown fountain pen, houses a very delicate mechanism, which can easily go out of commission if it is not handled or cleaned properly. A small paint cup designed to hold a limited amount of color, is attached to the brush. Through suction created by air pressure, the color is drawn from the cup and expelled as a spray through the nozzle of the brush. The various valve adjustments for controlling the volume of air, and for regulating the quantity of color, also govern the size of the spray. It is possible to get a spray as fine as a pinpoint or as broad as a wash. The Thayer and Chandler, Paasche, and Wold companies, foremost manufacturers of airbrushes, place at the disposal of artists a large assortment of airbrush instruments to meet the varying needs of the profession.

Airbrush Color. Practically any finely ground color, if made thin enough, can be used with the airbrush, but the best results are obtained when colors especially formulated for airbrush work are employed. Such colors are free from impurities and are of the right consistency to be used straight from the bottle.

Masking Mediums. A frisket sheet is a specially prepared paper out of which the airbrush mask or stencil is cut. It serves to shield portions of the art work from the spray of the airbrush. It is better than ordinary paper for this purpose because it is thin and transparent, making it possible to trace cut the mask directly over the drawing without a pencil tracing. Its water-repellent coating keeps the paper from curling or wrinkling when water-soluble ink or paint is sprayed over it.

In lieu of special frisket paper, a workable mask can be cut out of any substantial paper or cardboard and held in place with the hand like a decorator's stencil or else weighted down in position. Some artists prefer to brush in a rubber cement preparation over those portions of the drawing to be protected from the spray. When the airbrushing is finished, this rubber cement resist can be peeled off without injury to the drawing.

Of course, there are cases where the masking medium can be dispensed with altogether. No frisket is needed when the entire background is to be sprayed in. Similarly, when it's only a small area that is to be retouched or shaded by airbrush, the spraying can be done without a frisket. The spray can be made so fine that it will not fan out in a wide arc but will hit only that certain part of the drawing.

Frisket Knife. Though the frisket can be cut with a razor blade or a sharp pocket knife, the task is made easier when the handy type of frisket or stencil knife is used. This is a small, keen-bladed stylus equipped with a vise control adjustment for interchangeable blades. The X-Acto line of stencil knives offers a wide assortment of styles to choose from.

Procedure for Airbrushing.

1. Cover the entire sheet of frisket paper with a thin deposit of frisket cement or ordinary rubber cement diluted with benzine.
2. Place the frisket paper, cemented side down, over the card to be airbrushed. Pat the paper lightly so that it will adhere to the cardboard.
3. With the knife, lightly cut out of the frisket paper the shapes corresponding to those portions of the poster which are to receive the spray. When the frisket paper has thus been trace-cut, peel away the paper within the cuts so that a frisket or stencil is formed.
4. Place the card to be airbrushed in an inclined position on a drawing board or easel. Fill the color cup attached to the airbrush, and try out the spray on a test sheet, making any necessary valve adjustments. The brush is held in a horizontal position and gripped like a pen. To manipulate the airbrush, press the lever that starts the flow and direct your spray to the areas to be airbrushed. For a very fine spray, limited to a concentrated area, hold the brush close to the cardboard. To cover a larger area with a fuller spray, move the brush farther away from the

board. Manipulate the brush with a slightly circular motion and do not concentrate it for too long a time in one spot. If a more intense tone is desired, respray the same area more than once, but give each application a chance to dry lest the wet particles of color merge to form blotches.

5. When the color is dry remove the frisket. The cement on the frisket paper acts only as a temporary adhesive which allows it to be peeled off without any trouble.
6. Clean the brush. Run clear water or alcohol through the brush until not a trace of color remains in it. Be certain the instrument is thoroughly clean inside and out.

SPRAY TECHNIQUE

An atomizer or ordinary insecticide gun filled with diluted paint can also be used to spray color onto a drawing. Friskets or stencils, similar to those used in airbrushing, protect portions of the drawing from the paint. Since the opening or nozzle of a spray gun is not adjustable, the size of the spray cannot be regulated. Nor is it possible to produce subtle tones with this means, because the hand pumping action necessary to produce the spray causes an intermittent, unsteady flow of paint.

SPATTER TECHNIQUE

Spatter work produces a coarser and more irregular surface texture than is characteristic of either the spray or airbrush techniques. Only a few simple household tools plus a certain amount of dexterity are needed. Fill the bristles of a discarded toothbrush with diluted paint. While holding the toothbrush horizontally, scrape the bristles lightly with a match, a nail file, or other such common implement. By agitating the bristles, a spatter, composed of myriads of specks of paint, is produced. However, it is difficult to direct the spatter with any great degree of accuracy.

Practically the same results can be achieved by rubbing the paint-saturated bristles of a toothbrush over a wire mesh screen which is held horizontally just above the part of the drawing to be spattered. Here too, it's a trick to make the spatter go right where you want it, but with experience, the thing becomes manageable. A frisket may or may not be used, as the case warrants it.

STIPPLE TECHNIQUE

Stippling is a means of introducing a gradation of tone in a given area by applying individual blobs of paint with a brush or other device. The density of the resulting tone is determined by the size and proximity of the paint dots. The technique is slow and tedious but is rewarding in the interesting texture and tones that it yields. Stippling can be done with a sponge or rag as well as with a brush. This technique is faster and has a quality all its own. A small sponge is dipped into paint and worked out on a scrap of cardboard. It is then dabbed over parts of the drawing, leaving a reticular deposit of color with each dab. The texture of the sponge, the consistency of the paint, the amount of paint carried, and the pressure exerted will influence the kind of stipple you get.

DRYBRUSH TECHNIQUE

To get a drybrush effect, charge an old lettering brush, preferably one with split or uneven bristles, with fairly heavy paint and work it out on a piece of blotting paper until very little paint remains in the bristles. The brush is manipulated with rather vigorous sweeps and is lifted with an upward swing as the end of a stroke is reached. Lines painted with a semi-dry brush are neither sharp nor definite. They show a ruggedness and dry edge, most noticeable at the end of strokes where practically all of the meager charge of color has been depleted. It takes a real artist to make drybrush work seem casual and unstudied, without giving the impression of carelessness or slovenliness.

ROSSBOARD TECHNIQUE

Rossboard is a special type of illustration board which comes in several varieties of rough-textured finishes. The surface is made up of minute elevations and depressions giving it the proper "tooth" for holding pencil and crayon work. The crayon, held lightly as it is drawn across the board, leaves its mark only on the elevated parts of the pattern and does not reach into the depressions. Thus, a line or tone drawn upon Rossboard is automatically broken up into myriads of little dots. With experience, it is possible to get an infinite range of tone values varying from intense unbroken black through the entire scale of grays. It all depends upon the pressure exerted on the crayon. The heavier the pressure, the darker the area.Those areas entirely untouched, constitute the "highlights" or "whites."

A photoengraver's line cut can be made from a Rossboard drawing without any trouble. The reproduction will match the original, dot for dot in every detail. Rossboard will take solids as well as tones, but while it is ideal for charcoal drawing effects, it cannot be used for watercolor washes. When a definite unbroken solid is desired, it is attained by exerting heavier pressure on the crayon or better still, by brushing in the solid with ink or paint.

CRAFTINT TECHNIQUE

A black-and-white drawing made for one color reproduction can be given additional tones by introducing dots, parallel lines, crosshatching, stippling, and so forth. These effects can be obtained automatically through the use of Craftint Illustration Board. This patented sheet, which appears white in color the same as any illustrator's stock, has within it a chemically impregnated pattern.

After the line drawing is painted in, the area where an intermediate tone is desired, is brushed over with a chemical fluid which brings to the surface the pattern heretofore invisible. When one drawing is to carry two distinct tones, use is made of a special Craftint sheet known as Doubletone, with its own specific chemical.

The tone derived chemically on Craftint board simulates a mechanical Ben Day effect such as is seen in the shaded areas of newspaper drawings, cartoons, and so forth. In fact, many of the newspaper line drawings where tonal values appear are made with these patented sheets.

SCRATCHBOARD TECHNIQUE

Scratchboard work resembles a wood engraving in its emphasis on sharp contrast between black and white. When the special paint-coated cardboard needed for this technique is not available, it may be prepared in the following way. The surface of any smooth, clay-coated cardboard can be covered with black paint or India ink, and allowed to dry. On this black surface, the design can be scratched out with a needle, a stylus, or other such tool. It will be found that the ink or paint scratches off easily, every scratch revealing the pure crisp white of the original board. The scratchboard technique lends itself admirably to inexpensive line cut reproduction, it makes the most of one-color printing, and is an excellent illustration medium.

PHOTOGRAPHIC TECHNIQUES

Paste-up. The art of photography can be applied to poster design in many ways. The most direct application, of course, is the use of a photographic paste-up in place of a hand painted drawing or design. In making a layout for such a poster, a photograph—in most cases a close-up—is worked into the composition together with hand painted or type-set copy. Photographic paste-up posters seem to run an even race in popularity with those that feature hand painted illustrations treated with photographic realism. Though this type of presentation can degenerate into a stock formula for poster designs, it may be saved from such a fate through interesting layout variations. The choice of the photographic model, the perspective, the size of the photograph, and the position it occupies on the poster in relation to the other elements are all variables which make one poster different from another.

Photomontage. To a creative artist, photography is an eloquent medium with unique poster possibilities. Photomontage—a multiple photographic study—consists of a number of different photographs so selected and mounted as to convey a total impression. For example, on a travel poster advertising popular winter sports, the spirit of the winter games may be epitomized in symbolic and startling glimpses of skiing, tobogganing, skating, and so on. Herbert Matter's photographic posters show how closely related are the magic of photography and the art of poster design.

Photomontage may borrow the tricks of surrealism in which the composition as a whole is not a literal presentation but a conceptual impression blending fantasy with reality. The poster artist is of necessity restricted in the use of such interpretations. He cannot expect to dip far into the well of the subconscious and draw from it illustrative material which will have meaning to a wide audience.

Collage. Collage is the use of any material fitted together into a unit in a composition. The more unusual the elements that comprise the unit, the more interesting the results.

The composition may consist of pieces of varicolored paper fitted together to create a form of pleasing design. It may consist of parts of entirely different photographs apparently bearing no relation to each other but which, when united in a composition, take on strange forms that are startling to behold yet convey a concept succinctly. It may consist of different materials or substances selected and shaped so that each contributes its textural quality and three-dimensional nature to the total effect. The creative design may be an actual clay model; something carved out of wood or soap; a figure cut out of cork or rubber; any composite design made with patches of cloth, wool, or other material.

Q. Would you say it is permissible to use more than one technique on a poster?

A. The word "permissible" is not listed in the dictionary of creative art. The artist is "permitted" to use any technique or combination of techniques as long as the results are good. The superb work of Joseph Binder, one of the chief exponents of flat poster treatment, shows how well the ephemeral quality of the airbrush can be used to advantage to set off a severe, geometric pattern. In fact, if you analyze the work of such famous poster artists as Bernhard, Carlu, Cassandre, Shepard, Steinweiss, and others, it becomes evident that it is not only "permitted" to use more than one technique, but it is recommended.

Q. In planning a poster, how does one decide which technique to use?

A. The decision is based on two considerations: the aesthetic and the practical. Perhaps I should have mentioned the practical first. The artist must know the technical requirements of each of the important printing processes, and be able to so adjust his painting technique to production specifications that it will give the best printed results with the least trouble to the printer. The aesthetic consideration resolves itself to the question of which technique will best carry out the thematic concept of the design.

Q. Can an oil painting, a wash drawing, or other fine art medium be employed on a poster?

A. Yes, any style of painting may be used. With modern printing methods it is possible to duplicate mechanically most any kind of art work. However, from the art point of view, the most impressive poster technique is one which lends itself more to a virile design than to a pretty picture.

Q. How about a cartoon style illustration on a poster? Would you say that a cartoonist can make a good poster artist?

A. It is hard to say whether a cartoonist would make a good poster artist, but we do know that a cartoon can be a dynamic ornament on any poster. I have seen excellent posters where a blow-up of a well designed cartoon was the central pictorial attraction. The work of Hoff, Soglow, Steig, Szyk, Taylor, and other famous cartoonists and caricaturists have frequently appeared on posters. I do not know, however, whether these artists were responsible for the complete layout of the poster or whether they merely supplied the cartoon.

Q. If an artist evolves some unique painting technique, can he copyright it so that no one else may imitate his style?

A. No. A painting technique may not be copyrighted. An entire poster, an illustration, a drawing, trademark, or other original design can be copyrighted. The fee is two dollars and applications for exclusive rights to an original design are filed with the United States Patent Office in Washington.

Q. We know that poster paint dries with a dull mat finish, yet we have seen many posters where the paint seems to be sort of glossy. How is this finish attained?

A. To get a slightly eggshell or glossy finish, the painted areas have to be burnished. This can be done by placing a sheet of thin paper over the poster, and rubbing over it with the back of a spoon. Another way is to rub a wad of absorbent cotton or a soft rag lightly over the painted area. The burnishing treatment removes traces of the powdery residue which usually becomes evident when poster paint dries. It makes the painted areas appear smoother, and helps to hide any evidences of uneven distribution of paint. Need I add that before you do this burnishing the paint must be bone dry?

Q. We have always found it difficult to manage a light color over a dark one. What suggestions can you make to help us solve this problem?

A. The easiest way to solve this particular problem is not to create it. Plan the painting so as to avoid putting a light color over a dark one. But where it cannot be arranged differently, it is advisable to paint in the lighter area first and then to "cut in," that is, paint around the light areas with the darker color. However, "cutting in" is not always feasible, especially where the lighter areas are tiny or delicate. Wherever it becomes necessary to brush in a light color over an area painted with a dark color, try not to repeat your strokes. Going over the same stroke more than once tends to dissolve the color underneath, which in turn adulterates the lighter shade. If two coats of paint are necessary for better coverage, wait until the first coat is perfectly dry before applying the second.

There are some colors which are almost impossible to cover. I have in mind turquoise blue, cerise, some magentas, and other "lake" colors that are strong in dye content. If you attempt to apply white paint over a background painted in turquoise, the white will invariably turn a bluish green as it dries. Going over the white will not help.

Q. What will help?

A. Practically nothing. The best thing to do is to anticipate that condition, and either avoid a "lake" color background or paint in the other color first. There is one other possible solution. If a "lake" color background it must be, and you can't "cut" it in, paint it with sign painter's Japan color thinned to the proper consistency with turpentine. When that is dry, regular white poster color can be applied without a bleeding reaction. Or the procedure may be reversed. The background may be painted in poster colors and the lettering in Japan colors. Japan paint and poster paint do not affect one another.

Q. But don't you find that poster color over a Japan-painted surface often refuses to "take" and that the oily surface seems to interfere with the adhesion of the poster paint?

A. Yes, that sometimes happens but it can be remedied. Next time you have that trouble, stroke your brush on a piece of soap each time you palette it. The soap mixed in with the poster color does the trick.

Q. Then why not recommend this method unreservedly? What is the objection to such a procedure?

A. Mainly, because the average poster artist is unaccustomed to working with sign painter's colors. The paint does not flow so easily; it has a tendency to leave a ring or halo on the card around the painted parts; it dries slower and does not have as nice a finish as poster color does.

Q. Do you ever employ colored inks for your posters?

A. I rarely use them. Although colored inks possess a singular luminosity, they are transparent and entirely too watery for use with the brush. I do use black ink which is suitably opaque for lettering or for designs intended for line cut reproduction. I might add that India ink should not be painted over an area that has been covered with opaque poster color because the ink will crack off almost as soon as it dries. However, poster color can easily and safely be applied over any area that has been coated with India ink.

CHAPTER SIX

MAKING A POSTER

THIS is a description of how to go about making a poster. It is by no means offered as a prescription or fixed formula. Deviations in the routine depend upon the type of poster the assignment calls for, the established work habits of the person who makes the poster, the conditions under which the job is performed, and so on.

If the publicity committee of your club or organization asks you to get up a poster, you will naturally not devote so much time nor thought to it as you would in undertaking a commission to create a poster for one of J. Walter Thompson's big accounts. You know that your club will accept (with proper tribute to your genius), any poster you hand in. We are not concerned with that type of work at present. Our interest in this chapter is with the type of assignment you may expect from an important client or a large advertising agency. The following outlined procedure, in order to be more meaningful, is based on a hypothetical situation.

Let us assume that the advertising director of the National Conference of Christians and Jews commissions you to design a poster for the annual observance of Brotherhood Week. We shall not go into the questions of a fee or a deadline, taking it for granted that all that has been amicably settled, and you now have the "go ahead" to proceed with the job. Your specification sheet reads:

SPECIFICATIONS: Reproduction trim size: 14″ by 20″, upright
Border: 1″ white border, 4 sides, within trim size
Copy: Brotherhood Week, February 11-17
By-line: Sponsored by the National Conference of Christians and Jews
Additional Copy: Optional
Printing Process: Offset lithography
Illustration: Appropriate design or picture
Art Technique: Optional
Colors: Optional

RESEARCH WORK

Research should precede drawing. The first thing to do is to try to find out what appeals to the client. An examination of the posters used in previous years will reveal something about the client's taste and standards. This preliminary survey will, at the same time, steer you away from submitting an idea which by sheer coincidence might be identical with one already used. These coincidences do happen.

As you look through the assortment, you discover that some of the more popular symbols and design motifs have already been used. One poster shows a crucifix and a Star of David side by side. Another has a colossal statue of Lincoln, the Great Emancipator. Still another features a close-up of two hands clasped in friendship. All these you decide not to repeat, no matter how significant their original appeal. The problem is becoming more difficult. It seems that every idea that suggests itself as a symbol of brotherhood has already been exploited.

The next phase of research involves going through your reference library. The poster artist owns–in addition to a classified "morgue" of selected clippings–a collection of art magazines, trade journals, American and foreign art books and art annuals. Most artists are proud of their collections and the unique systems they have evolved for making reference material easily accessible. Some of the more popular books and magazines found on the average poster artist's shelves are *Production Yearbook*, the series of *Art Director's Annuals*, back copies of *A-D Magazine*, *American Artist*, *Signs of the Times*, *Art in Industry*, the valuable but now rare *Gebrauchsgraphik*, *National Geographic*, *U. S. Camera*, as well as a collection of poster anthologies and books dealing with design and the graphic arts. No art library is complete without some of the splendid commercial catalogues and house organs such as *Westvaco Inspirations*, *Direct Advertising*, *Better Impressions*, and *Paper and Design*. These publications are usually kept intact; they are not looted for individual clippings. A good morgue of clippings (indelicately referred to as a "swipe file") is indispensable to an artist. Every professional has this indexed collection of pictures of animals, foods, sports, costumes, means of communication, modes of transportation, and so forth. The clippings naturally reflect the artist's reference needs, and they in turn, are determined by his field of specialization.

Well, you browse through your source material at random. You are not planning to pilfer anything. You are concerned primarily with getting your brain activated, and the best way to do that is to explore your treasure of books and catalogues. Closing your eyes in meditation will not help. It might lead only to your falling asleep. Nor will you find inspiration projected as a vision on the ceiling. You might instead become absorbed in the antics of a fly and follow its trek across the ceiling, down the wall, out of the window, and into the summer sunshine. This idle visual excursion might lead to some pleasant thoughts about going fishing, and the trouble with that thought is, that it may become an irresistible impulse. At any rate, you will have wandered off the subject entirely. So the best thing to do is to keep alert and engage in an active search for a definite cue to start you off on the right track. In the meantime, the blank paper of your sketch pad stares you in the face, pleadingly.

EARLY SKETCHES

Don't make the mistake of becoming inextricably involved in research. Time is flying. Pick up your pencil and start putting something down on paper. While browsing through one of the photographic journals, you chance upon an interesting photograph of a statue of Moses. It's an awe-inspiring statue of Moses carrying the Tablets of the Law. Here's the germ of an idea—something for your first "thumbnail" sketch. You jot down a rough facsimile of the figure, making it occupy the greater portion of one of the little 3 inch by 4 inch rectangles marked off on your sketch pad. Across the top you indicate in rough lettering, Brotherhood Week. Across the base of the statue you inscribe February 11-17. Elsewhere, you quickly stump in the by-line "Sponsored by the National Conference of Christians and Jews." The dummy lettering merely indicates the tone and position of the finished lettering.

If you should decide to use the Moses photograph as a source of inspiration and for reference material, you can do so without a feeling of impunity. You are not guilty of a "swipe." To the best of your knowledge, neither the sculptor nor the man who photographed the statue intended it to represent the symbol of brotherhood. What the picture did was merely to set your mind to thoughts of Moses as a prototype of brotherhood. There is no law against that.

Well, it's an idea, but your search is not yet ended. By browsing further, you may come across something that offers other possibilities. An original idea may be awakened not only by direct association but also by opposite association. Here is a typical example of this psychological phenomenon. You may be thumbing through an old issue of *Gebrauchsgraphik* when you come across a war poster in which a menacing-looking battle sword is used as the central theme. Something clicks in your brain as you look at this symbol of war and you think of a laurel wreath. All right, that is idea number two. You sketch in a large laurel wreath, and within its open branches you inscribe in Old English lettering "Brotherhood Week." You do not concern yourself with the rest of the copy; you'll find space for it later. It's the main idea that counts right now.

Give up? Not yet. You also record an idea of a large American flag unfurled to serve as a background for the copy. Next you experiment with a figure of Thomas Jefferson, then a close-up sketch of ants working together harmoniously at some common task. Somehow or other, though you now have five thumbnail sketches, you feel that your quest is not ended. Frankly, you are not satisfied. In abstractedly turning the pages of a recent copy of *U. S. Camera*, your attention is attracted to an interesting microphotograph of a very heavy rope—the kind used for ship's rigging. Only a small section of rope, greatly magnified, is shown running diagonally across the page. Here is something that definitely appeals to you. This symbol of tying things together well typifies the spirit of brotherhood. But a rope, for all its symbolic potentialities, is such an unbeautiful thing to paint on a poster. You don't even consider it worth putting down on paper, but still you can't dismiss the impression it has made on you. In the process of cogitation, as your gaze strays off, you become aware that your wrist watch band is composed of a series of interlocking links that form a decorative chain. The thought strikes you that a chain would be an ideal alternate for that rope idea which still lingers with you. Excitedly you make a thumbnail sketch wherein the chain is used as the central theme. You do not show a chain in its entirety; you dramatize the effect by concentrating on several powerful-looking links, slanted across the rectangle, and running off the sides.

And now for the weeding out process. You review your little gallery of sketches and instinctively feel that the chain idea is best. You get the opinion of others, too, if you are broad-minded about the thing. The following is the agreed opinion of all the critics of your one-man show. The Moses idea, while good, is a bit too sectarian. It might be thought to slight one-half of the Conference of Christians and Jews. The laurel wreath is quite satisfactory, but it has too frequently been used as a symbol in peace posters. The sketch with the ants in it now seems absurd—definitely out. The flag idea stresses patriotism more than brotherhood, and while patriotism is a virtue, it's brotherhood that is the present objective. Jefferson, too, is dismissed. The role that he played in American history is not well known enough to the general public for his presence to be associated with the fraternity of mankind. We are back to the chain motif, and that is easily the most logical candidate.

THE COMPREHENSIVE SKETCH

The next version of the chosen idea is made full size and dressed up in color. This is called the color comprehensive. Going back to the specification sheet, you note that the poster will be lithographed, which means that you are at liberty to use any painting technique and any number of colors. You also note the fact that you are free to use additional copy.

You make a fairly careful layout of the poster, showing a close-up view of several links of a chain. To add significance to your symbol you stump in the words "Brotherhood, Democracy's Strongest Link." Getting the word "link" into your coined slogan is fortunate, because it helps to tie up the copy with the picture. You don't neglect to give due prominence to the date. And way at the bottom of the sketch, you letter in—not too well but so that it can be easily made out—"Sponsored by the National Conference of Christians and Jews." This wording appears as a long base line of lettering. The comprehensive is now colored in: picture, lettering, and all.

This "compo," as it is affectionately called, can be rendered in one of several ways. It may be done with crayons or poster colors on illustration board, or with pastel crayons on tracing paper which is then mounted onto board. If the client is familiar with your work through previous associations, it is not necessary to go to any great length to present a finished-looking compo. He knows what to expect from you and can anticipate the finished results from a "visual," which is more detailed than a rough thumbnail sketch yet not so complete as a trim-looking compo.

When your comprehensive is finished, you have something tangible to show to the customer, and though you would like to have it OK'd as is, it will be no calamity if the client indicates changes or rejects the idea. The actual making of the compo has taken no more than two or three hours of your time. So, fortified with the finished comprehensive and lots of hope, you are on your way. Lest we forget, you have not discarded the other thumbnail sketches you made for this job. They are now neatly tucked away in your pocket, just in case the customer should reject the comprehensive and want to look over some of the other ideas.

GETTING THE CLIENT'S APPROVAL

It might have been better to have this heading read, "Getting the Client's Opinion" because he does not always approve. However, let us see how this brotherhood poster is received.

The person in charge of advertising for this inter-faith organization is a woman. After exchanging the usual greetings and salutations, you unpack your comprehensive and hesitatingly put it up for inspection. She looks at it —and is delighted. She calls in several other people who all think it is a fine idea. They especially like the copy you wrote, admiring its excellent slogan value. Knowing a woman's propensity for changing her mind, you decide not to show her any other idea sketches. "Let well enough alone," you say to yourself.

One of the gentlemen in the admiring group has a suggestion to make. Wouldn't it be a good idea to incorporate the Statue of Liberty somewhere in the composition? Upon considering the suggestion you say that it would be a grand idea; not just to "yes" the gentleman, but because you really agree with him. You indicate on the compo the position and size of the famous statue. You sketch it in so scaled down in size that it seems to recede miles away into the distance. The effect is startling. Contrasted against the diminutiveness of the statue, the links seem to have grown in size, they seem to have become perfectly colossal. The appearance of the statue adds dramatic perspective to the composition. What is more, the Statue of Liberty unmistakably identifies America as the land of brotherhood.

With the comprehensive now fully approved, you return to your studio to go ahead with the poster.

MAKING THE FINISHED POSTER

Get final reference material. The really difficult part, the creative phase, is over. Now it's purely technical. Before you make the finished painting, there are several things you will want to check with your reference files. Going through your morgue, you pick out some pictures of massive chains, also a good photograph or two of the Statue of Liberty. Having authentic reference material will add confidence to your drawing. One may not always find just the right photograph no matter how extensive the clipping collection. It is for this reason that many artists have taken up the camera to obtain firsthand documentary material.

Decide on the work size. The specifications call for a 14 inch by 20 inch poster, held upright, allowing for a border within the trim size. Trim size refers to the dimensions of the card after it is cut. Allowing a 1 inch border on all sides reduces the actual working or painting area to 12 inches by 18 inches. You can work s.s.—that cryptic appellation stands for Same Size—or whenever it might prove more convenient, you may work on a larger scale. Any size is OK as long as you retain the fixed proportion. You decide on s.s. in this case because the actual dimensions offer a convenient working area.

You get a piece of illustration board considerably larger than the required size. Starting off with a larger card allows for trimming off the edges which are bound to become soiled and fingermarked during painting and handling. On this card, you square off and pencil in a rectangle measuring 14 inches by 20 inches. Within that boundary, allowing for the margins, you lay out an area 12 inches by 18 inches. This is the work size.

Trace the design on the illustration board. Now you make a careful sketch of the corrected drawing and trace it onto the illustration board. If you dig too hard, the point of the tracing pencil will create deep grooves in the cardboard so bear down just enough to leave an impression but not to engrave the outlines.

Get your paints matched and mixed. When you decide upon the colors you match and mix them in sufficient quantities, preparing a little more of each color than you think you will need. It is better to have some paint left over than to run short before the job is finished. Rematching certain shades is a difficult if not an impossible task.

See to it that the paint is thoroughly mixed to a free flowing consistency. Once the paint mixture is properly prepared, it should be just right for brushing and should not require adjustments during the process of painting. As a final checkup, each color should be pretested to see how it dries. The little scrap of cardboard on which you make the color test should be identical with that used for the actual poster, since the color is somewhat affected by the surface upon which it is applied. For the most part, colors when dry look flatter, duller, and lighter than when wet.

Begin your painting. The large areas you paint in with a three-quarter- or one-inch, chisel-edged brush, preferably the kind sign writers use for single stroke lettering. The brush is worked rapidly in long even strokes so that the entire painted area will dry almost simultaneously. Where the work is outlined with a small brush and then filled in, it is best to do the filling in quickly while the painted outlines themselves are still wet. Doing it this way helps to prevent streaky or lumpy brush marks around the outlined areas. Painted areas that dry lumpy not only look sloppy but they also have a tendency to crack and chip. To assure an even-toned area, free from brush marks and lumpiness, no paint must be allowed to accumulate in puddles.

With the major background and illustration areas painted in and dry, you now proceed with the details of the lettering. In a good grade of poster paint, the lightest of colors is sufficiently opaque to cover any dark color upon which it may be applied. If a line of light green lettering is to appear on a black panel, the background is first painted solid black and allowed to dry. The lettering is then painted over that. Most lettering is handled in this direct way, that is, the lettering is superimposed over the background. On the other hand, when the lettering is very bold—as in some of the blocky Gothic styles—it may be "cut in." This means that each letter is given shape by painting around it, while the letter itself is left in the background color. For tiny lettering or fine detail, it is unprofessional to use the "cut-in" technique, which is time consuming and doesn't always yield good results.

Getting the poster ready for presentation. Even after the poster is all painted in, you are not quite ready to deliver it. It must be dressed up for its debut with the client. First of all, guide lines and fingerprints are removed with art gum or kneaded eraser, leaving intact only those lines which indicate the trim size of the poster. The card is then trimmed slightly on all sides to get fresh-looking edges. You may further enhance the appearance of the finished poster by matting it. But whether you go to that length or not, really doesn't matter. The important thing is to present a job that is immaculate. A paper flap, hinged on the back of the card and covering the entire front surface, will protect the painting and add distinction to the presentation. If you are really proud of the job and feel that the work does you credit, you may sign your name neatly within the painted area of the poster. (Hint: the poorer the art work, the larger and fancier the signature.) And now, with the finished poster in your portfolio, you are on your way to the client.

Getting the final OK. Judging from the nice reception your compo got and from the neat and professional way in which you handled the finished painting, you should have no trepidation about unveiling the poster before that august audience, the client. The gentleman who made that suggestion about the Statue of Liberty will be particularly pleased to see that his good idea has been incorporated and with such telling effect. You have accredited yourself completely and have at the same time made good friends and a worthwhile contact.

In cases not so hypothetical as this, the final painting may require a few minor corrections, but it is seldom necessary to re-do the entire painting if the artist has guided himself by the client's comments, suggestions, and instructions at the time when the comprehensive was shown and discussed.

Q. Just how important is the morgue? Shouldn't an experienced artist be able to draw without having to copy from photographs and other pictures? We know a principal of a large art school who is against the idea of the students of his school using photographic aids.

A. The morgue or clipping file is becoming increasingly important to artists of today who draw from photos as much, if not more so, than from the actual model. And there are good reasons for this. It isn't always practical to get a model to pose for an extended period of time. Nor is it always possible to go on location, say to India, when you need to draw the Taj Mahal. How can an artist fulfill an assignment to draw an authentic model of a stratoliner if he has to rely purely on his memory or imagination? What does the average artist know about things generally foreign to his interest and experience? It may interest you to know that one of our famous artists who is known for depicting jungle scenes with convincing realism, has himself never been south of Boston. All he knows about life in tropical jungles he has gleaned from photographic reference studies.

As for that school principal's stand, I have no doubt that he is fully aware that it is an accepted professional practice to draw from photos whenever there is an advantage in doing so. Students at school, however, in order to get their roots firmly planted in the fundamentals of drawing, composition, and anatomy, should learn to draw from life and memory and not become incurably dependent on photographs. That most likely represents the principal's point of view, and with that I heartily agree.

Q. In maintaining a clipping file, how do you classify the clippings? We mean, if you're filing a picture of a sailboat, for instance, do you put it in the category marked Navigation, Transportation, Ships, Sailboats, or what?

A. That problem has always been a headache to artists. If you have an elaborate collection, here is one suggestion by which you can keep track of your clippings. Take that item of the sailboat. The original clipping may be put in any one of the files you mentioned. In the other logical files, such as the alternates you suggested, you may insert either a quick tracing of the picture or else an inexpensive photostatic copy of it. On each of these duplicates you jot down a memo telling you where the original copy is to be found. In this manner, the same item is represented under a number of different logical headings, and yet the original, because of this system of cross-indexing, is always accessible.

Q. What recourse is there for the artist who has not gathered an extensive reference file? Where can he find reference material outside of his own studio?

A. The New York Public Library has a splendid compilation of indexed clippings classified according to subject matter. Its picture collection boasts of over a million clippings and offers a source of authentic reference material on any subject. You may study or copy the pictures right then and there or borrow a limited number of them on your library card. A good many libraries, as well as some museums, maintain similar collections, although not of such magnitude.

Q. We have no more definite questions, but could you give us any general hints or suggestions that might prove helpful in planning and making posters?

A. At the moment, I can think of only two suggestions. The first one is concerned with what production men call "makeready." This means that before you start a job, you should anticipate and set up everything you will need to do the job in the most efficient way. What you don't need put out of the way —even out of sight. Leave nothing to stumble over on your way to answer the phone, nothing to roll down the inclined drawing table, or to topple over accidentally as you move about. One pays a heavy price for inefficiency.

The other hint is: Learn to finish what you begin. Don't get in the habit of being so severely critical that nothing you do pleases you. If you continue to tear up your work, you kill all incentive to start again, for you preclude a similar fate for your repeated attempts. The importance of this maxim was brought out in a recent poster competition conducted among students of an art class. The race had narrowed down to six finalists. Five of these "experimented" with grandiose ideas for posters but did not come through with a single finished one. They kept tearing up attempt after attempt. The sixth student—by no means the most talented artist of the group—undertook something within his means, finished it to the best of his ability, and submitted it on time. His poster wasn't a masterpiece but since he was the only one to submit anything before the deadline, he won. The others lost by default. The complex of dissatisfaction, of destruction before completion, is difficult to overcome. But it can be done if you undertake something within your means and finish it. Don't let your reach exceed your grasp.

CHAPTER SEVEN

WHAT EVERY POSTER ARTIST SHOULD KNOW ABOUT PRINTING

ARTISTS who work for commerce and industry, unlike individuals engaged in the fine arts, do not paint for their own pleasure. That is, they have someone to please besides themselves. They have obligations to a very practical-minded "patron," the client, who does not believe in art for art's sake. The client is interested in the artist's painting only as a means to an end. He knows that nobody sees the original art work but he hopes that everybody will see the print, so it is the print with which he is really concerned. The artist is financed by the client and must respect his interests.

While the artist is not expected to supervise production (and for all we know, the printer would consider it an intrusion), he is expected to plan his art work in such a manner that it will be completely acceptable for reproduction. The commercial artist must work hand in hand with the people who make the plates and do the printing. He must, by the very nature of that relationship, have a working knowledge of the major printing processes and their manifold technicalities.

The best way to learn to appreciate the printer's problems is to share them. It would be a good idea for commercial art schools to require all students to serve an apprenticeship in a printing or engraving establishment some time before they graduate. Such an internship might well be made a prerequisite for certification. In fact, that is the plan followed by some of the better art schools in Europe. By means of such an arrangement the student artist sees at firsthand how exasperating it can be to deal with artists who are ignorant of the *modus operandi* of the reproduction processes. An artist who is unfamiliar with the requirements, may in all innocence introduce numerous technical difficulties. Some may be insurmountable. Others might have to be solved arbitrarily by the printer, with a possible disappointment to both artist and client. In the feverish brain of the printer exasperated by a piece of art work which some ivory-tower artist designed with a profound ignorance or complete disregard for the technical requirements of the medium, there looms a vision of a Hereafter, where the erring artist is made to do penance by being forced to solve the printing problems he has himself created.

An important item on the artist's specification sheet is the reproduction process to be used. In addition, the artist should be informed as to how many will be printed, on what kind of stock, and where the work is to be posted. Information such as this is vital to intelligent planning of the art work. Given these production notes, the artist must hew close to the line to make it possible for his design to be reproduced as planned without any technical complications.

Suppose a poster were specifically scheduled for reproduction by silk screen. In ignorance of the limitations of this process, the artist proudly delivers a painting in beautiful blended tones, subtle washes, and an unchecked range of colors. The silk screen printer takes one look at this masterpiece—and has a fit. He cannot handle a job of this kind because his process can be used only where the design is painted in a limited number of clearly definable flat colors. And so it is with every other process—letterpress, lithography, gravure, or photogelatin. Each graphic art makes its own demands in treatment and technique.

It is well to remember that the public judges an artist's ability by the print that bears his name, not by the quality of his hand painted original. In many cases the reproduction is so poor compared to the original, that the printer shows the artist a real kindness by omitting the signature.

All printing processes fall into one of three major categories: relief, planographic, or intaglio. This distinction is made on the basis of whether the design on the printing plate is raised, flat, or sunken. A good way to remember the distinction is to call to mind the three levels of transportation: elevated, surface, and subway.

Relief Printing refers to the processes of making prints from a plate which bears the design in relief. The rubber duplicating stamp is a familiar example of such a plate. So are the type punches on a typewriter. Ink applied to the printing block will cover the high surfaces but will not reach into the low areas. When paper is pressed against the plate, it will take on an ink impression of the raised portions only. Printer's type, photoengraver's line cut and halftone plates, linoleum blocks, woodblocks, and rubber plates work on the principle of relief printing.

Planographic Printing, of which lithography is the best example, is a method of printing from a perfectly flat surface, part of which has been so treated as to accept ink, the rest to reject ink.

Intaglio Printing is a method of printing from a plate the surface of which is broken up into microscopic cells of varying depths. It is the ink held within these cells that is drawn out and deposited on the paper during the process of printing.

With the above cursory classification serving as groundwork, let us pause to examine each of the printing methods a bit more fully.

RELIEF PRINTING

The principle of printing from relief plates was known to Chinese woodcut artists a thousand years ago, yet oddly enough, woodcuts and linoleum printing blocks are today made the same painstaking way as they were by those early Orientals. The present use of hand-cut blocks is relegated to the fine arts. For commercial purposes, most relief printing plates are engraved by photomechanical means.

LINE CUTS

A line cut is the name given to a type of photoengraved metal plate which is used to reproduce line drawings. While the term "line drawing" suggests art work done in pure line, it also denotes drawings rendered in any black-and-white technique, whether it be solids, stipple, spatter, or crosshatching.

A drawing that is to be reproduced from a line cut may be made larger than it is to appear in the finished print; it may be made the same size; or it may be made smaller. Usually the original drawing is made large enough to allow for carefully worked out details. It should not be made so large as to require reduction to less than one-half or one-third its original size. Excessive reduction causes thin lines to drop out and closely inked lines to smudge. To get a preview of what it will look like when reduced, the work may be viewed through a diminishing glass. A magnifying glass is used to discern irregularities in sharpness and other discrepancies, so that the art work may be touched up before it is sent to the engraver.

When the photoengraver gets the copy—the original art work—he adjusts his camera to get a clear, well-focussed picture in the specified size. He "shoots" the copy and subsequently develops the negative. Here in brief is what happens once the negative is made.

A flat sheet of metal, usually zinc or copper, is covered with a chemical which is sensitive to light. The negative is placed in contact with the sensitized metal sheet and thus exposed under a powerful arc lamp. Light passing through the transparent parts of the negative strikes the sensitized surface of the metal and brings about a change in the coating. All areas of the coating which have been struck by the light become insoluble in water; those parts shielded from the light remain water-soluble.

After the plate is exposed, it is coated with a special adhesive ink and then held under a faucet of running water. The sensitized coating and the ink on the unexposed areas wash away, while both the sensitized coating and the ink on those areas which had been exposed to the light, do not wash away. When pulverized resin—technically known as "dragon's blood"—is applied over the plate, it adheres only to the inked areas. Upon heating, the resin melts; when cooled, it forms a protective acid-resist film covering the areas originally exposed to light. Those areas, as well as the back and sides of the plate which are similarly treated with adhesive ink and "dragon's blood," become impervious to the action of nitric acid.

The plate is immersed in an acid bath, which etches or "bites" away the unprotected metal, to an extent depending upon the number of bites and the length of time the acid is allowed to do its work. After the last bite, the plate is washed in cold water to remove all traces of nitric acid. A hot lye solution dissolves the dragon's blood. What was originally a smooth sheet of metal is now an etched plate composed of a depressed surface and an elevated surface.

Larger sections of the depressions may be routed out with a hand tool, to make these areas so deep that absolutely no ink will reach them when the plate is inked for printing. We are not finished yet. While the rest of the process is not spectacular, it is nonetheless important. Since printing machines for relief or letterpress work call for plates of a certain gauge, the thin line cut plate must first be nailed onto a wooden block of the required thickness. When this is done, the line cut is at last ready for the printer.

HALFTONE ENGRAVINGS

A halftone cut is the name given to a printing plate by which photographs and other pictures are reproduced in graded tones from light to dark. The distinguishing difference between a line cut and a halftone is that the former is used to reproduce a drawing in a single tone, and the latter reproduces work where there are variations in tone.

Upon close examination, a halftone printing plate will show a surface broken up into tiny dots uneven in size and unevenly spaced, but all of equal elevation. What appears on the print as a variation in tone is due to the difference in size and spacing of the dots which comprise the picture. Halftone work is in evidence in photographs for newspapers and books, as well as for most facsimiles of wash drawings, airbrushing, and subtle pencil sketches.

A halftone plate will reproduce the colors in a picture only so far as their relative color values are concerned. Such a print will be a one-color reproduction expressed in terms of light and dark, unless the three- or four-color process is used. But we are drifting ahead of the story. We should confine ourselves for the present to single-color halftone reproduction.

To make a halftone plate, the art work is first photographed by a camera which is equipped with a special screen. This consists of two sheets of glass, each of which is marked off with closely ruled, parallel hairlines. The two pieces of glass are so cemented together that the lines of one sheet intersect at right angles with the lines of the other, forming a fine mesh of squares. There are different grades of halftone screens for different types of work, ranging from 55-line (which means that there are 55 ruled lines to every linear inch) for printing on rough paper, to 175-line (175 ruled lines to the inch) for fine reproductions on smooth paper. Pictures reproduced in newspapers, for instance, are usually photographed through 65-line screens. This means that every square inch of such a screen has 65 times 65 or 4225 apertures. In a 133-line screen there are 17,689 apertures per square inch. If the paper to be printed on is smooth, it will permit the use of a very fine halftone screen, producing an impression in which the dots are hardly discernible. If the paper is rough, a less-fine screen must be used which, of course, means that the screen marks will be quite distinct on the print.

On account of the screen, whatever image is reflected through the camera lens is broken up into a mosaic of dots. The illusion of dark areas on the negative is created by large dots closely packed; light areas are represented by fine specks. No part of the picture comes out pure white or pure black. Once the negative is ready, the rest of the procedure for making a halftone plate is identical to that of making a line cut plate. The etched plate has a surface of innumerable metal dots that stand out in relief. On occasions where the contrast effect of pure white is desired, the extraneous screen dots are scraped off by hand. A print from such a plate is known as a "highlight halftone" because the white of the paper shows through unobstructed by any screen of dots.

THREE- AND FOUR-COLOR PROCESS

The halftone color process by means of which art work can be reproduced in full color, is based on the theory that all colors can be derived from the three primaries red, yellow, and blue. To get the photographic negatives for multicolor halftones, three shots are taken, each with a different color filter in the camera. The filters automatically separate and "extract" the three primaries inherent in the original art work. From the negatives, photoengraved halftone plates are made of each of the primaries. Printing these in sequence with their corresponding inks results in a reproduction which simulates the natural colors of the original, with but one major shortcoming—there will be no pure blacks. Whatever black appears has been obtained indirectly through the superimposition of the three colors. To give a more definite character to the print, a separate plate is made for printing black. This fourth plate marks the only difference between three-color and four-color process printing.

How is it that a color filter is able to select certain colors and be blind to others? A simple demonstration will make this clear. Let us say that there are three colored circles on a white wall—one red, one blue, and one yellow. If we look at the three circles through a piece of green celluloid, here is what we find: the yellow spot seems pale and lost, the blue one is equally weakened, but the red one comes through intense and blackish. Red is by far the most dominant of the colors as seen through the green celluloid. Repeating the same experiment with an orange celluloid, we find that blue predominates. With a violet celluloid, yellow predominates. In each case it will be seen that the filter is partial to its complementary.

The color filter in a camera used to prepare negatives for the multicolor halftone process, is nothing more than a colored piece of tissue, glass, or celluloid placed either in front of the lens or directly behind it. It comes in green, violet, and orange—the three complementaries to the primaries. The purpose of the filter is to detect a particular primary in the art work and register the values of that color on the negative. It doesn't matter whether that primary appears in its pure state or is found as a component part of another color.

A green filter is used to extract all the redness in the object before the camera—green being the complementary of red and not being responsive to yellow or blue. The green filter picks out the red and allows the negative to record it in terms of light and dark values. It is responsive not only to pure reds, but also to the presence of red in any degree in some other color such as purple, brown, or orange. An orange filter must be used to capture all the blue values. To extract all the yellow values, a violet filter is needed.

We must remember that the negative does not register colors as *hues* but as *values,* and consequently each of the three printing plates in three-color process work looks very much alike. Each one records practically the complete image. The only difference between the plates is the distribution of dark and light values within the picture. Since the plate is a graphic record of the value of the colors, it is up to the printer and the ink man to synthetically restore the chroma and hue. This is done by printing each plate with the respective primary ink. Printing offers no special problem, as each plate is handled like a regular one-color halftone. The usual sequence of colors is yellow, red, blue, and black, but the order may be changed at any time at the discretion of the printer.

In spite of its theoretical simplicity, three- and four-color process printing is fraught with fine technicalities. It calls for seasoned experience in color separation photography, care and skill in making plates, expert handling in getting the plates to register, know-how in the selection of inks, and the setting up of makereadies. Color process work, therefore, is reserved for fine printing and for large editions.

PLANOGRAPHIC PRINTING

Planographic printing refers to printing from an even-surfaced plate on which the design is neither raised nor sunken. Lithography and photogelatin are the most popular processes under this heading. The silk screen stencil process may also be included in this category.

LITHOGRAPHY

Let us, by calling attention to a common experience, look into the principle behind lithography. If you've ever watched rain falling on stone or pavement, then you surely must have noticed how any oily or greasy areas seem to shed the water. The application of this phenomenon to lithographic printing can be demonstrated in the following experiment.

Let us take a greasy crayon and with it draw or write something on a flat stone slab. When we then apply water to the slab, we find that the greasy crayon parts remain dry. Proceeding with the experiment, we roll fatty printer's ink over the entire surface of the stone by means of a rubber brayer. Here is what happens. The ink does not stick to the water-wet portions of the stone, it adheres to the crayoned areas only. Now we press a sheet of paper firmly against the stone. Upon pulling the paper away, we note that the crayon drawing has been transferred to the paper in an ink impression. Of course, the drawing is in reverse, but we'll worry about that later. What matters now is that we have seen how a perfectly flat surface can serve as a printing plate. All lithographic processes work on this dual principle: the opposition of grease to water and the affinity of ink to grease.

The discovery of lithography is ascribed to Alois Senefelder. The year was 1796. Senefelder, a musician by profession, had long been seeking a practical way of printing music sheets in quantity. For his experiments with different printing methods, he made frequent use of a stone slab which served as a good base for grinding inks. Around this stone a legend has been built up. The story is told that once Senefelder, not having pencil and paper handy at the moment when he needed to jot down a laundry list, made the memo on this stone with a stick of crayon. Always on the lookout for new printing possibilities, it occurred to him later to apply water to the stone and see what effect that would have on the crayon writing. When he noticed the water rolling off the greased parts of the stone, he was led to further experimentation to see whether that simple phenomenon could be the key to a new printing principle. Thus, although some people claim that he was looking for a new stone-etching process, he chanced upon something which seemed to answer his purpose better. He learned to control this newly found medium and with it, in time, he evolved the mechanics upon which the entire process of lithography depends.

The principle of lithography has remained unaltered since Senefelder's day; only the mechanics have undergone some changes. For commercial work, stone plates have been replaced by metal ones. This change was made, not because stone lithography did not yield highly satisfactory results. On the contrary, prints made with stone plates have not been surpassed in quality. The change was made only because the use of stone plates is commercially impractical. First of all, the type of stone best suited for lithography is heavy and unwieldy. A small stone 10 by 12 inches is about 2¼ inches thick and weighs approximately 30 pounds. A 30 by 40 inch slab can come to about 400 pounds. If you consider the enormous dimensions of an outdoor billboard poster, you can figure out for yourself the aggregate weight of the stones that would be required to produce jobs of that size. Then too, the spacious storage facilities litho stones require and the special care needed to prevent their cracking or chipping, constitute serious hindrances from the commercial point of view. We must remember that the fastest printing machines today work on the rotary cylinder principle which requires that the printing plate be curved around a cylinder. Since lithographic stones obviously do not lend themselves to such handling and since they have these other limitations, some suitable substitute had to be found. The answer was metal plates.

A study of the working surface of good Bavarian limestone, the kind used by Senefelder, revealed a grainy texture and peculiar absorbent quality in its make-up. These conditions have, as far as possible, been duplicated mechanically on the zinc and aluminum plates in use today. Metal plates combine many advantages. They are thin and comparatively light in weight; they can be bent to take on the shape of rotary cylinders; they are more durable; and they occupy very little space in storage.

There are two types of lithography: direct and offset. In direct lithography, the print is made by direct contact between the paper and the printing plate. The design is applied to the plate in reverse—as seen in a mirror. Referring to the hypothetical experiment with the crayon drawing on the stone, you will remember that the impression came out reversed. If the design is put on backwards to start with, it will come out right in the print.

In offset lithography, the printing plate prints first on a thin rubber "blanket," and that in turn offsets its wet impression on paper. Thus, offset work really amounts to a print of a print. The design is applied to the metal plate exactly as it will appear on the reproduction. It can be figured out easily enough that the impression reverses itself on the "blanket" and rights itself on the paper.

The procedure for making a lithographic plate is as follows: A thin sheet of zinc, aluminum or stainless steel is ground down by a special process to take on a pebbled textured surface. It is then washed to clear away all the pumice abrasive employed in the process of "graining" and at the same time, to remove any grease marks or fingerprints that may be on the sheet.

The design to be reproduced is either copied onto the plate by hand with tusche or is transferred to it by photographic means. For handmade plates, the lithographic artist first makes a key tracing of the design on the freshly grained metal plate, and then fills in the tonal areas with litho crayon or liquid tusche. He may use any technique on the plate that the original art work calls for—solid tones, lines, stipple, spatter, rubbed crayon effect, and so forth. The litho plate-maker must be an artist in his own right to be able to duplicate sympathetically the original art work. He must also be an experienced colorist, as it is up to him to so analyze the colors of the art work that the job will be printed in as few colors as possible.

For photographic plates, the original art work is photographed and a negative made from it—much the same as for a line cut or a color halftone. The metal plate is then given an even coating of a light-sensitive albumen solution and allowed to dry. The negative is placed in firm contact with the sensitized plate and thus exposed to light. Where the light passes through the negative, the chemical coating is hardened and made insoluble in water. This represents the image which will print. The coating which was shielded from the light by the negative is washed away. Once the image is on the plate—whether by manual or photographic means—the plate is then so chemically treated that only the image will have an affinity for ink. It is now ready for printing.

All lithographic presses are equipped with two kinds of rollers: one for spreading water over the surface of the printing plate, and the other for spreading a film of ink. The action of the rollers is so synchronized that the water rollers always precede those which carry the ink. Offset printing, although it does not produce as brilliant a color job as direct lithography, is faster and cheaper.

PHOTOGELATIN

A gelatinous substance will absorb moisture in proportion to the state of softness or hardness of the gelatin base. The softer the gelatin, the more moisture it can absorb. From the process of lithography, we already know that moisture and fatty ink do not mix. Let us relate these two principles and see how they form the basis of photogelatin or collotype printing.

The first step in preparing a photogelatin printing plate is to photograph the original art work. No screen is used in the camera, resulting in a negative that is in continuous tone—without dots of any kind. This is unlike the screened negatives used in halftone work where the image is broken up into innumerable dots. The negative is set in contact with a gelatin-coated glass or aluminum plate and exposed to light. The gelatin will harden in direct proportion to the amount of light that passes through the negative. After exposure, the plate is moistened with a mixture of water and glycerin. More of this mixture will be absorbed by the soft gelatin areas than by the hardened areas. As the ink rollers pass over the plate in the process of printing, more ink will cling to the dry and hardened parts of the gelatin than to the moist and soft parts. The tonal range in a print from such a plate reflects the infinite variations in the amount of ink sustained by the gelatin.

The susceptibility of the gelatin plate to variations in moisture must be vigilantly controlled. Every precaution must be taken to keep the room in which the printing is done moisture conditioned, so that the gelatin will not dry out nor take on excess moisture, but will retain its fixed state of absorbency regardless of any changes in outside humidity.

Practically any type of art work may be reproduced with the photogelatin process: photographs, wash drawings, oil paintings, or simple black-and-whites. The process is at its best when used to reproduce jobs where photographic facsimiles in quantity are required. Photogelatin is not good for runs

NATIONAL

Progressive Proofs of 4 Color Printing Process. Courtesy of National Brewing Co.

MARYLAND'S
AMBASSADOR
OF GOOD CHEER

NATIONAL Premium
NATIONAL
BEER
BREWED AND BOTTLED BY THE NATIONAL BREWING CO., BALTIMORE 24 MD.

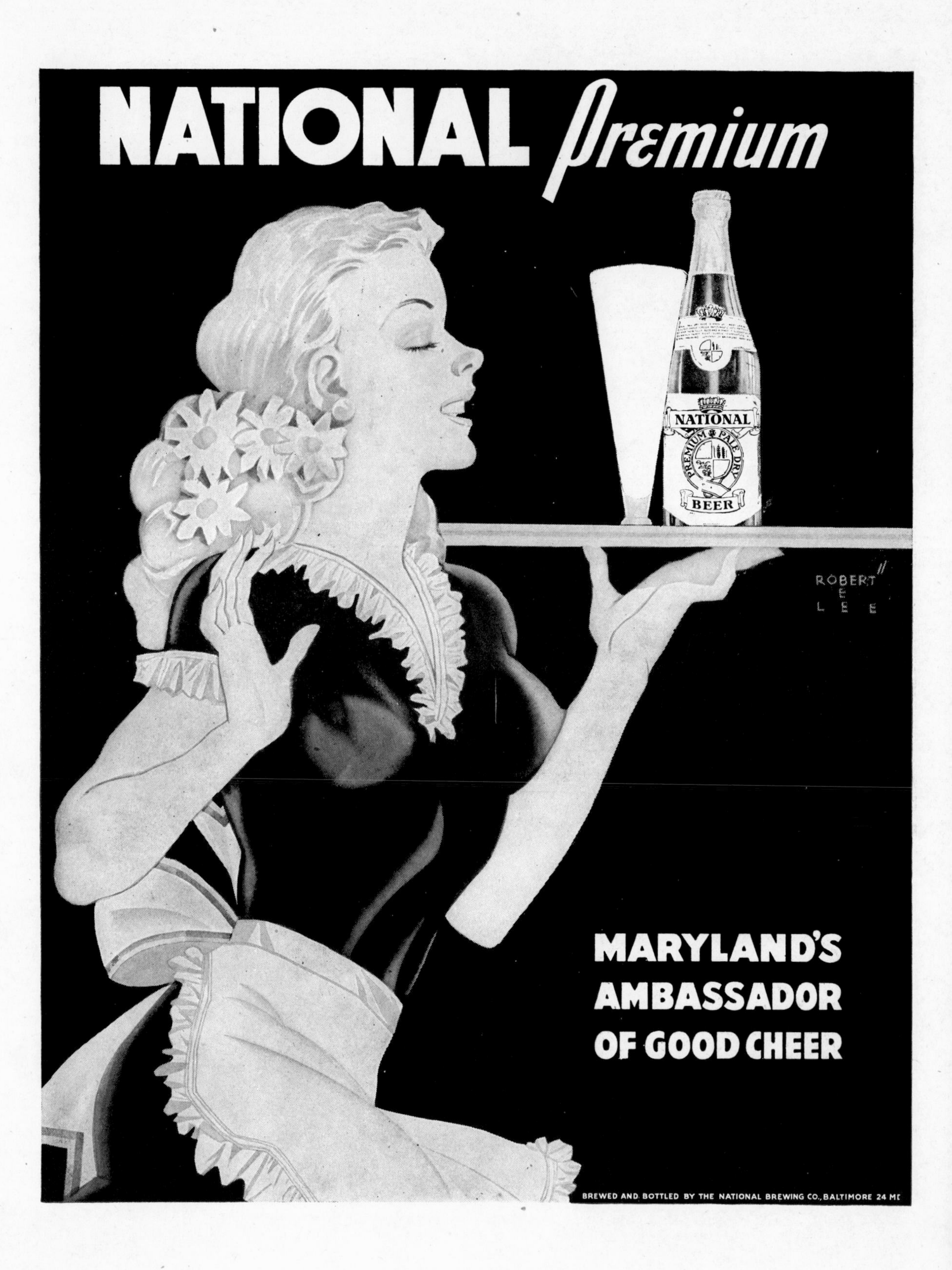
NATIONAL Premium
NATIONAL
PREMIUM PALE DRY
BEER
ROBERT E LEE
MARYLAND'S
AMBASSADOR
OF GOOD CHEER
BREWED AND BOTTLED BY THE NATIONAL BREWING CO., BALTIMORE 24 MD

NATIONAL Premium
NATIONAL
PREMIUM PALE DRY
BEER
ROBERT E LEE
MARYLAND'S
AMBASSADOR
OF GOOD CHEER
BREWED AND BOTTLED BY THE NATIONAL BREWING CO., BALTIMORE 24 MD

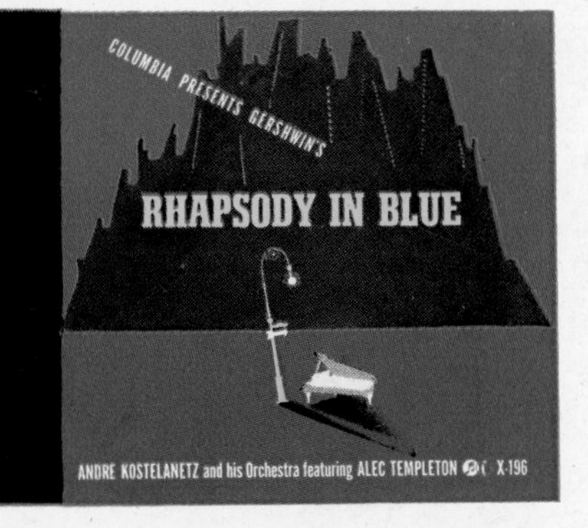

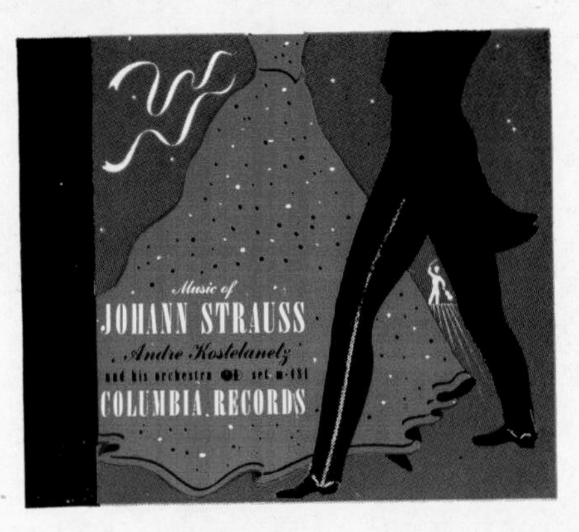

Record Album Cover Designs—Alex Steinweiss. Courtesy of Columbia Recording Corp.

that exceed ten thousand prints, or for anything larger than 40 inches by 60 inches.

SILK SCREEN

The silk screen method, based on the principle of the stencil, is ideal for flat-color poster reproduction. Since the stencil can be made to deposit an appreciable layer of richly-pigmented paint, a silk screen print has a hand painted impasto effect not obtainable with other processes which merely stain the surface with ink.

To better understand the modern silk screen stencil process, let us examine the stenciled markings on a shipping case. We notice that the lettering is made up of disconnected strokes. That is, there are little "breaks" in some lines, especially noticeable in O, A, and other letters which have isolated centers. These breaks in the print are caused by the small paper links which were used to hold the integral parts of the stencil together. Today, no connecting links of any kind are required. The silk screen stencil process, as the name implies, employs a silk fabric as a screen, and the stencil is affixed to this screen.

A piece of resilient silk known as bolting cloth is tightly stretched and tacked on a rectangular wooden frame. Bolting cloth, woven of fine strands of silk crossing each other at right angles, is porous, so paint can seep right through the holes of its meshwork. In order for the paint to penetrate faster through the mesh, a rubber implement known as a squeegee is used. The squeegee is scraped across the silk, and in crossing, pushes a layer of paint through the screen and onto whatever paper or card may be directly underneath it. So far the screen is "open," and paint can pass through over the entire area. To form a stencil, part of the screen is blocked out with some film-forming liquid such as glue, shellac or lacquer. The portions left open on the silk correspond to the shape of the design to be printed. Since the component elements of the stencil are held in place by the screen, the need for connecting links has been completely eliminated.

The typical silk screen printing unit consists of the squeegee, the silk-covered frame, and a board or flat table to which the frame is so attached that it can readily be raised and lowered. The board upon which the printing is done is equipped with register guides so that each card can be placed in a fixed position under the screen for the printing of each successive color. Because of the simplicity of the printing unit, it is an easy matter to construct special units to accommodate jobs of any dimensions. Signs, posters, and banners measuring fifteen feet across have been silk screened in one piece.

The process is one of the few commercial graphic arts which has not been mechanized. In the same factory building where huge rotary presses roll out thousands of impressions per hour, you may find a silk screen shop blissfully operating with homemade stencil units and hand squeegees, turning out two hundred to three hundred impressions per hour. For this reason, silk screen ceases to be practical for editions exceeding ten thousand prints or so, unless there is some other compensating reason for its use on a particular job.

This process, as every other, has individual production requirements. Every distinct color that appears on the original requires an individual stencil and a separate run. If a poster is designed in six colors, six stencils will have to be made and the cards will have to be run six times. Although most silk screen work is done with heavy opaque paint, when it is expedient for the sake of economy, the printer may use transparent paints. When one transparent color is printed partly overlapping another, three colors are obtained with the two printings. This overprinted color, however, does not always exactly duplicate the artist's original as well as when each color is matched and printed individually. Unless the artist co-operates closely with the printer, and guides himself by a color chart showing the results of overlapping the different combinations of colors, it is best to confine himself to fewer colors, and have each matched and printed separately.

The best silk screened posters are those wherein the art work is so rendered that all areas are flat and distinct, in real poster style, avoiding vague color boundaries and over-refinements in technique. The silk screen printer can do some tricks with blending and shading, but it is a costly and inexact art, better left to processes which are suited to sensitive tonal delineation.

INTAGLIO PRINTING

Intaglio refers to printing with a plate which imparts its impression from a subsurface image. The intaglio principle is the basis for gravure, stipple engraving, mezzotint, and dry point etching. Of these, gravure is commercially the most popular. Photogravure, rotogravure, and colorgravure are merely distinguishing designations for the various forms of gravure printing. They differ in the manner in which the plates are prepared and in the printing procedure.

In attempting to describe the operational principles of some of the other printing methods, we made use of hypothetical experiments based on familiar experiences. We shall employ the same device here to explain the intaglio principle. Let us take a sheet of copper with a nice smooth finish and scratch a few lines in it with a sharp needle or nail. We now spread some ink over the entire surface of the copper plate and immediately wipe the inked surface with a rag.

This is what we notice: while the rag has cleared the ink from the surface, it has not removed whatever ink is lodged in the scratched-out crevices. When we press a sheet of paper firmly against the plate and pull it off, the paper comes away with an inked impression of the scratch markings which were on the plate. The transfer of ink to the paper was brought about by physical pressure and suction.

GRAVURE

Thus far we have not touched upon gravure—we have merely given the basis underlying all intaglio printing. The gravure principle is more involved. In gravure, the surface of the plate is broken up into depressions or cells which vary in depth and are responsible for the variations in tone within the print. The deeper cells hold more ink and make a darker impression. The more shallow cells hold less ink and make a relatively light impression.

To make a gravure plate, a photographic negative is made of the art work. The tonal values of this negative are by photomechanical means translated into a meshwork of cells engraved on a copper plate. In the printing operation, ink is rolled over the plate and then scraped off with a "doctor blade" which removes all the surface ink but does not disturb the ink imbedded in the cells. When the paper comes in contact with the plate, the pressure and suction transfer the ink from the cells onto the paper.

The finished print does not reveal the presence of the multitudinous cells that make up the honeycomb of the plate, because the walls which separate these cells are so exceedingly fine. As many as twenty thousand cells fit into every square inch of the printing plate. In the printing, the gravure dots run into each other and blur slightly, resulting in a pleasing, velvety impression in which sharp detail is somewhat lost. The gravure process is reserved for fine photographic reproductions where a soft tonal effect is more desirable than sharp detail.

FINISHING OPERATIONS

Because many posters and practically all window displays have to be mounted, trimmed, or die-cut after printing, it is part of the artist's responsibility to know something about these operations which contribute to the total effect of the finished job. With the exception of silk screen, most printing processes are suitable only for thin paper stock. This is the reason why displays or posters are printed on paper first and then mounted to cardboard of the required thickness. Nor is it possible for a printer to handle a sheet where the ink extends to the very edge of the paper. Therefore, where a "bleed" is specified, the artist must remember to "overdraw" or extend the painted edge one-quarter of an inch or so on all sides where the finished print will later be trimmed. The job is run on slightly larger paper and then trimmed to size.

While most posters are cut square or rectangular, those that are designed as window displays are frequently stamped out in some irregular shape by the process of die-cutting. The artist should have a fairly good idea of how this process works so that when called upon to create a display with an irregular silhouette, he can design his work to conform to the practical requirements of the die cutter.

When the die cutter gets the job, the first thing he does is to make his pattern by tracing the silhouette outline of the design onto a block of plywood about three-quarters of an inch thick and somewhat larger than the allover dimensions of the design. He then very carefully goes over the pattern with a jig saw machine so as to leave an incision in the wood, all along the outlines. It is in this incised track that the cutting blades will be inserted. The blades, (steel rules) used in die cutting, are long narrow metal strips sharpened on one side like a single-edged razor. Since they are thin and flexible, they can be cut up to workable lengths, bent to shape and then wedged into the grooves of the plywood, so that the cutting edge of the rule extends about one-quarter of an inch above the base. When pieces of sponge rubber are glued to the base snug up against the protruding rules, the die-cutting plate is ready for use.

The plate can be used in either a platen or a cylinder press much the same as a letterpress plate. As each sheet of cardboard is fed into the guides, and by the action of the press forced hard against the steel rules, it is instantly stamped through. The sponge rubber cushions mentioned before, by their springy action, help push the cardboard away from the blade each time a cut is made.

Theoretically, a die can be made for cutting out any shape. There are two reasons, however, why the shape of a display should be kept along simple lines. First, the die will be less expensive for a simple shape than for one which has complicated cutouts. Then too, it is generally more functional from the point of view of construction and utility to keep the shape of a display simple in contour. One does not have to be a cardboard engineer to understand why it would be impractical to design a display with a figure holding a long fishing pole extended well beyond the main body of the display. While such construction would, no doubt, add a realistic touch to the idea, it certainly would be inviting trouble. The extended narrow strip of cardboard would become a vulnerable element in the construction and would cause an alarming percentage of these displays to be bent or broken in the process of cutting, handling, or shipping. Many an ingenious though impractical display which is produced at great cost because of complications in production and a high average of spoilage, represents a total loss to the advertiser. A dealer thinks nothing of discarding even the most expensive display if he should break it in his hurried attempt to unpack and set it up in his window.

This little object lesson is but another reminder to the artist to be realistic and practical. The advertiser is not interested in how ingenious or lovely art work may look as it reposes on the studio drawing board; he is concerned with the finished job, how much it will cost, and what it will do for him.

Q. To begin with, how does the artist know which printing process to favor in the choice of his art technique?

A. Normally, the art director will tell the artist which technique to employ. If the choice is left to the artist, he must be guided by practical considerations. It boils down to a matter of dollars and cents. Let me give you an example of what I mean. Suppose an art director of an advertising agency came to you and said, "Mr. Designer, one of our clients has allocated 750 dollars to us for poster advertising. For that, he is interested in obtaining one thousand cardboard posters 14 inches by 20 inches, in color." From these facts it should be clear that you are not expected to render a 500 dollar masterpiece in oils or watercolors. Not only would such a bill for art work be ridiculously out of proportion to the total allotment for the job, but even if the art work were to be contributed absolutely gratis, the cost of printing a full-color reproduction of an elaborate painting would in itself exceed the client's budget.

Q. Going back to that example of yours, what technique and what printing process do you think should be used?

A. Personally, I feel that the silk screen process would be best for that job. For a modest fee, an artist could get up a simple and good-looking poster in a few flat colors, and then the cost of silk screening one thousand posters in several colors would also be well in keeping with the budgetary allowance.

Q. What other process besides silk screen might do for that job?

A. Offset lithography would be my second choice. It probably would cost a little more money to do the job that way because a run of one thousand is considered a small order for lithography. Then too, posters printed by offset are not so rich in color value as those that are silk screened.

Q. You seem to lean towards silk screen printing. Can you tell us why?

A. That is begging the question. I favor silk screen only where it can be most advantageously used. For depth of color value and for a true facsimile of a hand painted poster designed in a limited number of flat colors, there is no printing process that surpasses silk screen. It unquestionably has an important place in poster and display reproduction for short editions, but I would not recommend it for runs of 25,000 or 50,000 for the simple reason that lithography can handle a job of that kind much more economically. Every process has its place; the artist ought to know when each will best fill the bill.

Q. What process is employed to produce outdoor billboard posters?

A. The majority of those billboards not painted by hand are printed by lithography and some are silk screened.

Q. How can the lithographer tackle jobs of such mammoth dimensions?

A. There are those who specialize in this type of work. By means of a lantern slide machine the artist's small sketch is projected in an enlarged form onto a wall the size of a standard outdoor bulletin. On sectioned-off paper tacked onto this wall, a key line drawing is made of the enlarged image. The section sheets, bearing the key drawing, are sent to the platemaking department where the art work is duplicated on individual zinc plates, either by hand or photographically.

The lithographic platemaker, an artist in his own right, uses the key drawing as his guide in drawing directly on the plate, and refers to the artist's original color sketch for the delineation of tones and distribution of colors. What you see on the billboard is really the lithographic artist's conception of the poster artist's design.

Q. Is each section printed separately?

A. Yes. Each of the ten press sheets is handled as a job in itself. Depending upon the color areas, one sheet may require six printings, another seven or eight, another only two. It's a big job when you reflect that it takes a total of thirty to forty printings to produce the average twenty-four-sheet poster. Remember, too, that the sections have to be made to fit together just right to make a continuous design when the sheets are laid up on the billboard.

Q. Why is it called a twenty-four-sheet poster when it is printed only in ten sections?

A. Originally, when lithographic presses were smaller, it was necessary to print twenty-four individual sheets to make up the full-size poster. The name has persisted although today the presses are big enough so that only ten sections are needed to make up the standard size, which is 104 inches by 234 inches.

Q. How large, or rather how small, should the original painting for a twenty-four-sheet poster be made?

A. There is no set size. The artist can suit his convenience in this matter. Some convenient sizes are 27 inches by 12 inches, 36 inches by 16 inches, 45 inches by 20 inches. It makes no difference, as long as the length of the sketch is 2¼ times its height. In other words, the proportions should remain 2¼ to 1.

Q. What about the art technique? Are there any restrictions as to style, colors, and so forth, for billboard posters that will be reproduced lithographically?

A. No, the artist is free to use any style he pleases. Lithographers will accept work in any medium and technique: water color, oil, pastel, poster color, air-brush, photographs, or what have you.

Q. By what method are smaller billboards produced—the ones seen on station platforms, on the sides of trucks, and posted on wall panels near neighbor-hood stores?

A. The great majority of them are lithographed, but some of them are silk screened.

Q. Are they as standardized in size as the twenty-four-sheet posters?

A. Not quite. Subway platform posters or "one-sheets" as they are called, are 29 inches by 45 inches, though these dimensions vary a bit in different parts of the country. "Three-sheets" generally measure 40½ inches by 82½ inches.

While we are on the subject of standard sizes—the average advertising cards displayed in subway cars, trolleys, and busses are 11 inches by 21 inches. The 11-inch dimension is fixed, but the length may be 21 inches, 28 inches, or 42 inches.

Q. Here's another query along these lines. How are movie lobby posters printed?

A. Most of the large movie posters are printed by the silk screen process. It has been found that silk screen stencils are less costly than plates for other color printing processes, and that by overprinting with transparent paints, a poster printed in four or five colors can give the effect of eight or nine. Posters which call for a realistic enlargement of a movie "still" may be lithographed or collotyped. Occasionally, one poster may be the product of two or more different printing processes.

Q. Are posters ever produced by the letterpress process?

A. Small posters may be, but for larger sizes, it is cheaper to use another form of printing.

Q. Why?

A. Mainly because the making of large line cut or halftone plates runs into a lot of money. For example, a 5-inch by 9-inch simple line cut plate for one color would cost about twelve dollars. Larger-sized plates are proportionately costlier. Imagine how much the letterpress plates for a twenty-four-sheet colored poster would amount to. And that does not take in the cost of printing.

Q. Do you mean that if a poster were printed by letterpress, each discernible color would have to be printed from a separate plate?

A. Not necessarily. The job may be done with Ben Day screens or by means of the halftone color process.

A Ben Day is a transparent screen bearing an opaque pattern of dots, lines, dashes, or other textural effects. It is used to give the illusion of additional tones or colors without actually printing them. For example, if your poster consists of black lettering and a border of gray, one line cut can do the entire job. I'll explain how that is done.

There are all sorts of Ben Day screens and textures. From a photoengraver's booklet of Ben Day samples, pick out by list number the pattern you want for the border area. Rule in the lines of the border and indicate the number of the selected Ben Day screen. The photoengraver will so process the negative or the plate that the lettering will appear in solid line, while the border will be broken up in the specified textural pattern. A black impression from this plate will show the lettering in solid black while the border will appear grayish. No matter what color ink you use, the same tonal relationship will exist between the solid and the Ben Day.

You may rely on the photoengraver to introduce the specified tonal effects, or you may make use of transparent Ben Day films which you can lay over the original black-and-white drawing. These sheets, which are available in an assortment of different textural patterns, are thin enough to be easily cut out with a frisket knife. The pattern on the sheet can be scraped off in spots to serve as highlights within a tone. Recently a special artist's illustration board was perfected having an invisible pattern impregnated in the board itself.

But I am afraid I have been carried away a bit by the chemical magic of Ben Day. To return to the question of using letterpress plates for color printing of posters, I might say that where the high initial costs of the plates are absorbed due to large editions, letterpress halftone plates become practical for smaller-sized posters.

CHAPTER EIGHT

YOU MEET THE CLIENT AND THE COMPETITION

THEY tell about a certain man in New York who professes to know very little about music, but who nevertheless lays down strict orders to professional singers and trained musicians on how to render well-known musical selections over the air. This man's judgment is respected, or rather—obeyed; he happens to be the commercial sponsor of an important radio program.

There are such mighty and unseen powers operating in the commercial art field, too. They are the people who admit, almost boastingly, that they know nothing about art; they know only what they like or don't like. In paying homage to such an egocentric individual, many an artist is forced to sacrifice seasoned judgment for tactical expediency. Some of the more grotesque examples of poster advertising seen on American billboards are sad commentaries on the vanity and whimsicality of many a misguided advertiser. The client, the man who pays for the advertising, is in a position to lay down the law to the art director or to the artist if he deals with him directly. It becomes a trying task to co-operate wholeheartedly with a layman who labors under the delusion that somehow he possesses divine intuition of what is good, and that the professional artist, at best, is merely a technician who can follow orders.

Large advertising agencies have developed into complex organizations composed of specialists in the creative aspects of advertising, as well as technical consultants on consumer response to color, copy, and other stimuli of sales appeal. Tests, charts, and other material of elaborate research are prepared and analyzed before any sketches are made for an important advertising campaign. The effectiveness of the submitted sketches is tested and anaylzed. When all is said and done by the experts, it is not unusual for the client to pop up with an idea or crude drawing of his own, or something that his newly-acquired son-in-law has dreamed up, and insist that that become the keynote for the whole advertising campaign. In a way, that *coup d'etat* is a blessing in disguise to the exhausted staff. Once the client has committed himself to something definite, the battle is half won.

To satisfy the elusive wishes of one important client, several topnotch artists were recently called in by a New York agency to submit idea sketches for a proposed billboard poster. Each artist was given free rein to design something in his own technique which would appropriately tie in with the copy submitted by the client. Many sketches were submitted, but the client kept on rejecting them all. He could not be pinned down to any direct criticism. In desperation, one of the puzzled artists working on the project determined to do a little investigating into the character and background of the client. He learned that this individual had some years ago been the chief copy writer for a large organization, and his success in this capacity had obviously developed the complex in him that his copy was more important than any other element in the layout. The enterprising artist was glad to make this discovery. His next sketch glorified the copy above everything else. The prominence given to the copy pleased the client immensely, so the sketch, with one or two minor corrections, was at last OK'd.

We are not prepared to say here whether the final job was the better or worse for catering to the whimsicality of the client; we merely have cited a typical example of the influence exerted on advertising by those who control the purse-strings.

LET'S HAVE A LOOK AT YOUR PORTFOLIO

Art is one of the few professions where the practitioner can launch himself on a career without any official authorization whatever to certify the extent of his training or ability. Official sanction is required to practice law, medicine, teaching, accountancy. Even the truck driver or the barber needs some sort of license or permit to ply his trade. But not the commercial artist. It's anybody's right to hang out a shingle and go into the business. As a consequence, people who require the services of an artist, must check for themselves to ascertain whether he who says he can do the work really can do it. Therefore, the artist, especially the newcomer whose reputation is not as yet established, must, in applying for a new job, carry with him evidence of his professional competence.

The samples in your portfolio represent your claim of competence and should be carefully selected for quality of workmanship, appropriateness, timeliness, and neatness. This means that you must exercise critical judgment in reviewing your work, so that what is included in your portfolio is a true index of your best efforts.

Workmanship. As you examine material suitable for your repertory, bear in mind that it is wiser not to include any work that will call for apologetic explanations. If you are in doubt about that poster which would have been heavenly perfection itself, except for that accidental smudge of paint or that foolish mistake in spelling, don't jeopardize your chances on the slim hope that your interviewer will have a blind spot for such discrepancies. When in doubt leave it out.

Appropriateness. All samples which meet your standards of workmanship should be further checked for appropriateness. Will your art work be of practical interest to the potential client or employer? Will it show your usefulness in a specific capacity? If you are applying for a poster job in a display studio, don't stuff your portfolio with arty wash drawings, charcoal nudes, or other uncommercial pieces. It is better to present convincing evidence of your proficiency in the type of work in which that studio is known to specialize. You may, of course, should the occasion arise during the interview, say something about your versatility, but avoid giving the impression that you are nothing but a Sunday painter.

Timeliness. Your samples should reflect current styles and art techniques—unless antiquarian drawings happen to be your specialty. Don't be a Rip Van Winkle; see that your work looks up-to-date.

Neatness. Neatness is also of paramount importance in all commercial art work. The samples that you show around should look clean and crisp, free from fingerprints and other marks of carelessness or old age. Mount or mat each piece neatly, and protect the painted surface with a paper or cellophane flap.

There is another factor to be considered in arranging the portfolio. It is always far more effective to include originals than photographic copies because no photograph or photostat can fully reveal your technique or manner of working. Yet that is what the art director is trying to judge. The art director knows that a photograph does not tell the unvarnished truth. It makes it easy to camouflage defects and rough details in the original. What is more, a photograph distorts true color values. The only time photostats should be used is when the actual art work is no longer available or when it is too big to fit into the portfolio. If you have press proofs of any of your work that was used commercially, by all means add them to your samples.

As to the portfolio itself, don't put yourself at a disadvantage by sporting one that is dilapidated or unmanageable. A zipper case or a large spiral-bound album represent a departure from the conventional flap type and are both smart-looking and practical. Although traditionally black, there is no reason why the artist's portfolio cannot be in a more optimistic color. A colorful portfolio will add spring to your gait.

FREE-LANCING VS. A STEADY JOB

Whether you like the adventure of shifting with the trade winds as a roaming free lancer, or prefer the peace of mind that comes with knowing you have a steady job, will in the final analysis depend on what type of person you are. If you are generated by an independent, aggressive spirit, the chances are that you abhor the regimentation that is associated with the daily routine of a steady job. In that case, you will no doubt be happier doing free-lance work, where you can be more or less your own boss and make your own hours.

It's surprising how busy free lancers, working as many as twenty hours at a stretch, will still insist that they are "making their own hours." Such is the contented state of mind of the rugged individualist. From the realistic point of view, the free-lance artist is deluding himself to a certain extent when he claims that he is his own boss. Actually, the art director or the client, though not a hovering supervisor, is still the overlord.

At first, the free-lance artist operates as a one-man organization. He is his own salesman, artist, and publicity director. He must establish "accounts," say something about his own merits (with due restraint and modesty), negotiate the fee, go back to the studio and turn into an art department. When the art work is finished, he becomes a delivery boy and rushes the job over to the client. Should any changes be suggested (which would not be unusual), the artist may have to make a few more trips back and forth until the sketch is finally OK'd. No sooner has he mailed out the bill, than he prepares for another pilgrimage in quest of new accounts. Of course he hopes to get more work from this same source, but he can't afford to wait. He has to eat in the meantime. And so, portfolio in one hand, address book in the other, the itinerant free lancer is on his way once more.

There may be long stretches of time when no new conquests are made and there is not enough work from the old accounts to keep the artist profitably employed. It is this irregularity and uncertainty that make free-lancing such a risky proposition. There are points in its favor, however, which make it worth while for courageous souls to want to take that risk. The free-lance artist is virtually in business for himself. As for the risk he takes, it is no greater than the risk any man takes in venturing into business. And the investment in capital outlay is comparatively negligible.

The free-lance artist, whose reputation becomes widespread, will in time build up a growing clientele which will keep him busy without continued soliciting. The artist may then choose to employ an agent on a commission basis to "service" the old and make new accounts while the artist devotes all of his own time to the creative aspects of the art business. It is the job of the agent to represent the artist, follow "leads," make contacts, develop accounts, and in general to act as the liaison officer between the artist and his clients. This nucleus of two, the artist and agent, may expand to include apprentices and assistants, and eventually develop into a large organization with a growing list of profitable accounts.

Offsetting the potential fame and fortune of the free-lance artist, are the many advantages enjoyed by those who have steady jobs with an agency, art department, or studio. First, there is the relative tranquility and security that come with a steady source of income. Then too, most people agree that there is a stimulating influence in working side by side with others. Those who want to further their professional studies find that the more or less regular schedule of the average working day leaves time for them to attend advanced art courses, thus bringing their talents to fuller maturity through continued training.

Oblivion is one of the dread diseases that artists fear the most. But the ambitious artist employed in a large organization need not assume that he is doomed to inevitable anonymity. If he possesses the quality of leadership seasoned with experience, he can aspire to become an art director and actually attain that distinction at an early age. Many successful art directors are people in their thirties who have come up from the ranks.

WHAT TO CHARGE FOR FREE-LANCE WORK

The free-lance artist must be realistic in his estimate of the commercial value of his talents. Unlike the aesthetes of the Greenwich Village art colony, who look upon financial success with disdain, commercial artists do not think it a negative reflection on their art or ethics to be financially successful. The artist should be a good business man. If he was just not born that way, he should have an agent or partner who has business acumen take care of the business dealings.

There is no fixed scale of prices for creative effort. Quality of workmanship can be evaluated only subjectively; it cannot be weighed or measured like so much rice or cloth. In determining a fee, other factors besides workmanship must be taken into consideration. Some of these considerations are:

1. How many copies will be printed of the design I create?

Before a price is fixed, it is reasonable for the artist to make inquiries as to the anticipated circulation of his design. Where work is to be reproduced in large quantities, the artist's responsibility to the client is greater, and he must exercise considerably more care in every detail of his work. He should, therefore, expect to be remunerated accordingly. What is more, a big job can absorb a higher fee for the art work because when compared with the total investment, the art costs dwindle down to a relatively small item in the production budget.

2. Will my design be used for one specific job only, or will it appear repeatedly in future advertising?

Correlated with the question of the circulation of the design is the matter of permanency. While actually there may be no more work involved in creating a trademark, masthead, emblem, or other such permanent design, than there is in getting out a routine poster, the fee for such work is determined on an entirely different basis. The artist, considering the permanent value and greater service of his design, charges more for art work that the client can use again and again than for something which becomes obsolete after its one appearance.

3. How valuable is the account?

An advertiser who gives his steady patronage to an artist is entitled to special consideration in the matter of fees. On the other hand, a client who comes to an artist with only an occasional job, should be charged a somewhat higher price for the same work than one would normally charge a steady customer.

4. How much will it cost me in time and materials to plan and produce the job?

Although the work of the free-lance artist is not paid for strictly at so much per hour, there must be some relation between how long it takes to do a job and how much is charged for it. For an elaborate oil painting, involving long hours of careful planning and research, and days or weeks of actual painting, it is logical and justifiable to fix the fee in keeping with the time and effort expended.

In creative art, there is hardly any relation between the cost of materials and the fee for the finished job: five hundred dollars can be paid for a poster done on a twenty-cent sheet of cardboard. The beginner in art often makes the mistake of charging little for his finished product because the materials necessary to produce it happen to cost very little. It is how the materials are used, not how much they cost, that matters.

5. How does the job fit into my working schedule?
When the job is so much in a rush that it must be given priority over all other profitable assignments, the artist has to go out of his way and reshuffle his working schedule to get that job out on time. In view of that, it is only fair for him to expect a higher fee—commensurate with the upsetting of his routine. On the other hand, if he is given a flexible deadline enabling him to do the work more or less as a fill-in assignment, he can lower his fee a bit.

6. How do I rate in the profession?
A shrewd client may show an eagerness to commission a celebrated artist not only because his work is superior, but also because a well-known name carries with it a certain prestige and has a definite box-office appeal. The client likes to imagine that a famous artist's signature on the poster will be taken as a personal endorsement of the product advertised. It is this desire to be associated with the "great" that prompts some small but ambitious advertisers to go beyond their budgeted allowance and splurge on an ad in a big-time publication of the class of *Esquire*, *Life*, or the *New Yorker*. The artist in all modesty should be cognizant of the commercial value of his professional standing and know how much it is worth to those who seek his services for one reason or another.

In addition to these enumerated considerations, one must at all times rely on common sense and practical psychology in one's business relationships in the art field.

WHAT MAKES FOR SUCCESS?

There is no tried and tested recipe for success in the art field. In this respect, the art business does not differ from other spheres of human endeavor. It would not be at all difficult to cite examples of artists who enjoy a measure of success in spite of flaunting some of the rules of the game. It would, however, be much more helpful if instead of dwelling upon the exceptions to the rules, we attempt to categorize the positive attributes that spell success.

Workmanship. There is no denying that people with unusual talent have a decided advantage over less-gifted individuals. An art director, for instance, will tolerate a lot of nonsense and trouble from a genius. There are artists who drive art directors to despair by willfully departing from specifications, by demanding excessive fees, by outright defiance in many ways. And yet, these same art executives find themselves forced by circumstances to work with these undisciplined but gifted individuals. This apparently irreconcilable situation can be explained by the fact that good workmanship overshadows all other considerations.

Reliability. No matter what his other virtues may be, a commercial artist will in time alienate his business connections if he does not "measure up" in certain personality traits. The most important of these is reliability. Though there is usually no formal contract binding an artist with respect to the fee, date of delivery, and other specifications, a reliable artist will make every effort to keep his side of the bargain. Because time is such a valuable factor in planning and producing advertising campaigns, the artist is expected to deliver the job on or before the agreed deadline date. In spite of all good intentions and well-laid plans, unforeseen situations may arise during the course of one's professional experience, which make it humanly impossible to live up to commitments. Under such circumstances, the artist should give the art director ample notice to make other provisions to meet his production schedule.

Emotional Stability. There may be room for eccentricity in the Fine Art field, but the commercial artist must be consistent and level-headed. There are some artists who are capable of doing superior work only when the fancy strikes them—when they are in the mood. By the same token, they can without any apparent justification, fall down on some important job so miserably and and so unpredictably, that the work done at this low ebb of their inspiration in no way reflects their true talent. No art director can afford to indulge in this game of chance with them; the results are too unpredictable. An artist, if he is to enjoy a long period of success, must be an even-tempered, steady performer who can be depended upon to live up to an established standard.

Modesty and Agreeableness. When a man's attitude proclaims "I am the greatest artist in America," he arouses in others a strong impulse to disprove that claim. When he casts aspersions on the integrity or talent of a colleague, then he does not aid his own cause in any way. A fitting sense of modesty and a respect for one's colleagues and clients add to one's own prestige.

It should be pointed out that unless an artist possesses such unusual skill that he is the indispensable man for a certain job, the art director will give as much consideration to his personality and character traits as to the quality of his work. Whenever he can, the art director will liberate himself from a recalcitrant genius and will shift the work to a man who possesses the desirable social and ethical attributes to match the technical excellence of his art.

Q. We have heard of more than one obscure artist who began his rise to fame as the result of winning a poster contest. Would you say that contests are worth while?

A. Contests are indeed worth while—but mostly to the firm that sponsors them. While it is true that winning a national contest may call public attention to the work of an unknown artist and indirectly advance his career, don't ever lose sight of the fact that contests are conducted primarily for the benefit of the sponsor, not of the contestants. It surely smacks of exploitation when for a small money prize, an advertiser can set the brains and hands of hundreds of artists to work. This well-planned scheme nets him thousands of dollars worth of free advertising in newspapers and trade journals, plus a harvest of ideas—all for a cash award of less than half of what he normally would have had to pay for the services of one artist directly commissioned to do the job.

Q. Are there any official restrictions which govern contests? We mean, can anybody run a contest?

A. As far as I know, it's anybody's privilege to sponsor a contest. I have long felt that there ought to be some kind of law making a license mandatory for any commercial or social organization wishing to conduct a contest. Such official sanction should be granted only to worth-while causes where social good and not private gain is the objective.

Q. What is your attitude towards working on "speculation"?

A. That is one of those practices which ought to be made illegal. The man who talks you into submitting sketches on speculation is gambling—with your time and talent. He is in the act of working on your gullibility when the dialogue runs something like this, "This new product we're putting on the market will outsell Coca-Cola in no time. You play ball with us and work up sketches for our advertising campaign, and when the stuff clicks, we'll take good care of you." Watch out for those glib empire builders. Tell them you can't live on promises.

If you are propositioned to contribute art work on the promise of being handsomely remunerated if and when your designs are accepted, you need not feel mercenary if you ask a down payment of at least half of the promised fee. Then you and the client will be speculating on equal terms.

Q. When offered a job which will take little time to complete, do you advise taking the work home or using the proffered studio facilities and doing the work right on the spot?

A. My advice would be to work in your own studio. You cheapen yourself by adopting the practices of the itinerant vendor. Don't do business like the man who fixes your umbrella or sharpens your knife while you wait. Since most free-lance work is paid for on a flat job basis, it is better to work in the privacy of your own studio and not to dramatize your hourly earning capacity.

Q. In presenting your samples to an art director or potential employer, what do you say as you show your work?

A. The less you say the better. Let the man who interviews you do most of the talking. When your turn comes, be modest in your claims and do not try to teach him everything you know in one lecture. Speak with animation but don't act the part of a high pressure salesman.

Q. What do you think of the idea of getting someone to act as your selling agent?

A. If you can persuade someone to do it, fine. Bear in mind, though, that the agent must live on the commission he makes from selling your work. You must be an artist of proved ability and really must give your representative something to sell; otherwise your agent will not be able to meet the competition of superior talents, and may be forced to leave you for more profitable connections.

Q. What percentage is it reasonable for the representative to expect on the work he sells for the artist?

A. The customary commission is twenty to thirty per cent of the price he quotes for the artist's work. However, the arrangement you make with your agent is a private affair and the terms can be adjusted to be agreeable to both parties concerned.

Q. If the agent adds on his own commission, can he still meet the price of competing artists who do their own selling?

A. Indirectly yes, because the agent sells quality, not price. Since quality is intangible and cannot be measured in terms of dollars and cents, a small difference in price is overlooked if the standard of workmanship and the service warrant it. In general, I think it is an excellent idea for an artist to join someone whose business it will be to represent him in his relations with art directors and clients.

Q. Why is it a good idea?

A. Well, for two reasons. A setup like that is efficient and effective. The artist can accomplish much more if he is not compelled to leave the drawing table to peddle his wares. And the representative can usually do a better selling job and speak more freely in praise of the artist and his work than the artist himself can or should. The ideal representative is a good salesman, not just an order taker. He makes a fine appearance, has a pleasing personality, and makes friends easily. But let's not forget that these qualities alone are not enough to make you or him successful. He needs good art work to back up his sales talk.

Q. Does any agent represent more than one artist at the same time?

A. Yes, that is often the case, if it is agreeable to the artists concerned. Naturally the various people he represents are specialists in different branches of art so that no internal competition is created. One man may be a specialist in drawing foods, another in cosmetics, a third in lettering, and so forth.

Q. How does the so-called "art service" operate?

A. This is a more complex version of the kind of artists' representative setup we have just spoken about. It starts with a couple of artists getting together and hiring an agent to represent them in the trade. They all share all the expenses of maintaining a studio, telephone, delivery service, and other facilities.

There is another species of art service organized by an agent or group of agents whose function it is to sell work for a selected group of artists. On file at the office there are representative samples of each artist's work, a cumulative list of his clients, and a complete file of data on his background, training, and specialty.

CHAPTER NINE

WHAT MAKES A POSTER "CLICK"

WHILE there is no empirical way to evaluate the merit of a poster design (unless we refer to its tabulated effect on sales or some other equally calculable response), there are certain recognized requisites or principles of good poster design which must be followed to make a poster "click." In the critical analysis of a poster one should consider how many of these guiding principles the artist has incorporated in his design and how successfully he has done so.

THE CARDINAL PRINCIPLES OF POSTER DESIGN

Simplicity

The layout should be simple. Generally speaking, the fewer units into which a given space is divided, the more pleasing it is to the eye. A poster should not be too busy. We often see posters which present a bewildering spectacle of confusing elements. It is as if the designer labored under the theory that if a few elements or units were good, then a good many of them must be so much better. If one illustration or panel is impressive, then why not put in three or four? This is not unlike the reasoning of a spectacular theatrical producer who, when he saw an early rehearsal of his pageant production of "The Last Supper," asked the director for twenty-four Apostles instead of twelve—to make it really "colossal."

A fussy conglomeration of units, needless to stress, entirely defeats the purpose of the poster. The best posters are those in which the units are few and simple. It is much better to have one large illustration dominate the composition, than to have a group of smaller ones compete with each other for attention. The lettering too should be kept within bounds. If placed within a panel, the shape of the panel should be kept simple and in harmony with the other shapes in the composition. Not everyone possesses the talent to make a poster technically perfect, but one need not be particularly gifted to make it simple; one must only resist the temptation to complicate it.

The treatment should be simple. Not only should the layout represent a simple division of space, but each unit in turn should by its simplicity add to the singleness of effect. There should be a minimum of different painting techniques and of different lettering styles. Copy should be logically separated into thought groups and arranged in block units. Feature wording, by its size and placement, should be given prominence over incidental copy. Only when that which is unimportant is subdued, does the featured copy stand out prominently by comparison.

A simple and organized arrangement with few elements, techniques, and lettering styles will make even a heavily-worded poster tolerably easy to read.

UNITY

Unity is the relationship or kinship between the several elements of a composition. The various elements that comprise a layout must seem part of the same poster; they must hold together. There are several ways of getting unity on a poster.

Direct overlapping of elements. The most direct way to knit the elements together, is to make one touch or overlap the other. The illustration is often made to overlap or extend into a line of lettering. When there are four or five elements in the design and it is not possible to have them touch at some point, some other unifying device must be used.

Pointing Devices. An artificial device may be introduced to bridge the channels separating the component elements in a composition. Some of the most obvious ways of directing the visual flow that develop unity are the arrow, the pointing finger, the decorative dots or rules and other devices borrowed from the typographer's bag of tricks. Sometimes the flourishing tail of a letter is artfully extended to lasso a roaming unit in a composition. In these ways the eye is guided rhythmically from one element to another, so that the design is encompassed as a whole.

We are all familiar with the design where the advertised product is used as a pointing device. The fountain pen or pencil is aimed in the direction of the trade name or selling price; oil or some other liquid is shown flowing from a source at the top of the advertisement, down in a long unifying stream to the bottom where the company's name appears. Cough drops or pills are made to drop out of a container and in their descent, lead the eye over a prescribed course to the brand name.

Unity may be attained by making two elements of the design face or incline towards each other or in some other way optically span the gap between distant though related units. In a formal type of poster, where the elements of the layout are presented in a sequential arrangement without touching, overlapping, or pointing to each other, a strong border will help to convey a feeling of unity to the composition.

BALANCE

A poster may have unity without having balance, if the elements on one side are unified by one of the means described above, but if there are none on the other side to balance the combined weight. There are two kinds of balance: formal and informal. A wet ink spot on a piece of paper folded in half, will result in an accidental design that is perfectly matched–truly bisymmetric. In a poster based on such formal balance, an imaginary axis running through the center will divide the design so that one half will represent the mirrored reflection of the other. A composition based on formal balance is static and always safe. It suggests repose, tranquility, contemplation, but no action. It is decorative, but not dynamic, and does not motivate the onlooker to do anything because it does not do anything itself. When the artist strives for classic atmosphere and stability, a layout based on bisymmetric balance will best transmit that feeling.

Balance is really a matter of creating an equilibrium so that what is on one side of the seesaw will somehow equal what is on the other side. To convey a feeling of balance without resorting to "blotto" symmetry requires imagination and daring on the part of the artist. He must employ color, strategic placement of copy or illustration, typographical devices and other means, to equalize the forces. Informal balance, alternately referred to as occult or asymmetric balance, is dynamic in its appeal and is therefore more in keeping with the attention-getting objective of a poster.

THE SELLING POINT

The aim of a poster is to sell something–a product, a service, or a cause–and the aim should be clear. A poster should lead to action–immediate or eventual. The plan by which one hopes to reach this objective constitutes the idea or the selling point around which the copy and design of the poster are planned. The idea may be blunt; it may be expressed in a layout that is nothing more than a "blow-up" of the product, with copy which simply states, "Buy ——," or "Ask for ——," or "Accept no substitute for ——." Such bluntness or naïveté is impotent because it does not tell *why* the potential customer should do as he is told or how he would benefit by following the command.

A good poster, once it has buttonholed the man in the street, rewards him in some way for the time it has demanded of him. The reward may be in the form of entertaining him through a humorous situation, it may instruct him by presenting an interesting bit of information, or it may put him in a good frame of mind by flattering his vanity. So the idea of an ad may hinge upon a popular saying, a play on words, a slogan, a rhyme, an anectodal or dramatic situation, or merely a convincing statement of fact. However it may be presented, the idea or selling point should be perfectly clear.

Surprise

We were going to say that if a poster is to be the right kind of selling agent, it must deliver its message in some unusual and surprising manner. But then, every poster need not be a super-salesman. There are occasions when the tipping of his hat brings a salesman more results than a forceful slap on the shoulder. Institutional posters, through which the advertiser builds up good will and prestige by slow degrees, must, to add confidence to the message, exercise great restraint in their general tone, yet they play a big part in the promotion of the company's products.

When a poster is planned for a one-look audience, it must be made to attract attention to itself instantly. This can be done by some rousing element of surprise, so that even the casual passer-by will be jolted into taking another look. A dynamic poster stimulates an immediate emotional response by means of an aggressive color scheme, dramatic perspective, provoking layout, or unusual painting technique. There must be something new or startling.

A humorous or dramatic incident may be sufficient to attract attention. An anecdotal situation may be presented through the medium of a photograph, an illustration, cartoon, or symbolic design. The theme or subject matter may range from the ridiculous to the sublime. A typical example: a scene showing a henpecked husband who has made a night of it, stealthily sneaking upstairs in the wee hours of the morning. In his anxiety to get up there unnoticed, he fails to notice the cat which is asleep directly in his path. The beholder, by being made to participate in the action, will pause to survey the ad more completely.

Anything seen at eye level is not as interesting as the same thing viewed from an unusual vantage point, so a poster with its illustration drawn in some out-of-the- ordinary perspective, will evoke more surprise than one where the illustration is of a normal eye view. This urge to see the world from a different angle is inherent in human nature. It can be observed in the antics of children who take a curious delight in bending down to look through their outstretched legs at a topsy-turvy world. It has been taken into account by the motion picture industry which has developed the technique of the close-up, the long shot, the bird's-eye view, the snail's view, oblique view—any angle or view which dramatically departs from normal perspective.

Correlated with the idea of surprising perspective, is the matter of size. It is far more interesting to view things which are reduced to lilliputian proportions or are fantastically enlarged. Size is relative. We measure one thing by comparing it with another. To give the impression of largeness or grandeur to a specific part of a design, one should contrast it with another part, exaggeratedly tiny. Another way of giving the illusion of colossal proportions is to focus attention on a magnified detail or fragment of an object instead of showing it in its entirety. It's a trick so to relate the dramatic detail to the composition, that the detail seems to be larger than the poster itself.

Anything that suggests precarious or temporary balance immediately creates tension and suspense. We watch the tightrope walker's act with animated interest because we cannot help but participate mentally in his attempt to challenge the forces of equilibrium. We are somewhat similarly affected by a poster layout where the lettering or illustration is slanted dynamically and forcefully. The observer is more inclined to reach out mentally to something tilted than to a package or product firmly planted on its base.

The element of surprise in a poster may be wrought also by a painting technique or style that is surprisingly new and different. The typographical technique of an artist like Lester Beall is as refreshing as it is unique. The photomontage style of Herbert Matter will for a time (until it becomes public property through imitation), continue to attract attention.

WORKMANSHIP

Though it is difficult to say how much a superior painting technique contributes to the success of a poster, it is a definite fact that most people are agreeably affected by a piece of work that is well rendered. By rendering, we do not mean to include the idea or the layout. We limit our consideration here to the quality of workmanship judged from a perfectionist point of view. Is the artist a master of his medium? Is he a good designer and draftsman? Is he an expert letterer? To sum it all up, is he a skilled technician?

It is understood that the individual elements comprising a poster may be rendered beautifully without adding up to anything. Unless there is an idea behind it, a poster may be all dressed up but get nowhere. Conversely, a poster may have all other qualities–idea, simplicity, balance, unity, and surprise–but if the quality of workmanship is poor, the poster may be ineffectual. The ideal poster (and there are very few that fall into that category) possesses all six of the cardinal requisites mentioned in this chapter. Let us bear these criteria in mind in studying the collection of posters which appears at the end of this book.

BIBLIOGRAPHY

Agnew, Hugh E.
OUTDOOR ADVERTISING
McGraw-Hill Book Co. 1938

Ashley
LINE DRAWING FOR REPRODUCTION
The Studio Ltd. 1941

Biegeleisen, J. I.
THE A B C OF LETTERING
Harper & Brothers 1940

CAREERS IN COMMERCIAL ART
E. P. Dutton Co. 1944

Binder, Joseph
COLOUR IN ADVERTISING
The Studio Ltd. 1934

Birren, Faber
COLOR IN MODERN PACKAGING
The Crimson Press 1935

Blair, Lawrence E.
PRINCIPLES & PRACTICE OF SHOW-CARD WRITING
McGraw-Hill Book Co. 1937

Carlyle, Paul and Oring, Guy
LETTERS AND LETTERING
McGraw-Hill Book Co. 1938

LEARNING TO LETTER
McGraw-Hill Book Co. 1939

Cavanaugh, J. Albert
A HANDBOOK ON LETTERING
National Process Co. 1939

Charlton, D. E. A.
THE ART OF PACKAGING
The Studio Ltd. 1942

Clemence, Will
MANUAL OF POSTERCRAFT
Blandford Press Ltd. 1939

Cooper, Austin
MAKING A POSTER
The Studio Ltd. 1938

Day, Harold Holland
MODERN BRUSH LETTERING
Signs of Times Publishing Co. 1931

DeLemos, John Thomas
PLANNING AND PRODUCING POSTERS
Davis Press, Inc. 1943

Downer, Marion
BE AN ARTIST
Lothrop, Lee and Shepard Co. 1941

Dwiggins, W. A.
LAYOUT IN ADVERTISING
Harper & Brothers 1928

Friend, Leon and Hefter, J.
GRAPHIC DESIGN
McGraw-Hill Book Co. 1936

George, Ross F.
SPEEDBALL TEXTBOOK
C. Howard Hunt Pen Co. 1941

Goudy, Frederic W.
THE ALPHABET AND ELEMENTS OF LETTERING
University of California Press 1942

Graves, Maitland E.
THE ART OF COLOR AND DESIGN
McGraw-Hill Book Co. 1941

Greer, Carl R.
ADVERTISING AND ITS MECHANICAL PRODUCTION
Crowell, Thomas Y. Co. 1931

Hohlwein, Ludwig
LUDWIG HOHLWEIN AND HIS WORK
H. C. Perleberg 1922

Holme, Geoffrey
LETTERING OF TODAY
The Studio Ltd. 1937

Kadel, George W.
AIRBRUSH ART
Signs of Times Publishing Co. 1939

Kauffer, E. McKnight
THE ART OF THE POSTER
Albert & Charles Boni 1925

Longyear, William
TYPE SPECIMENS FOR LAYOUT, PRINTING, AND LETTERING
Watson-Guptill Publications 1940

Luckiesh, Matthew
LIGHT AND COLOR IN ADVERTISING AND MERCHANDISING
D. Van Nostrand Co. 1923

Marinaccio, Anthony and Osborn, Burl
EXPLORING THE GRAPHIC ARTS
International Textbook Co. 1942

May, Don
101 ROUGHS
Frederick J. Drake Co. 1942

Mayer, Ralph
ARTIST'S HANDBOOK OF MATERIALS AND TECHNIQUES
Viking Press 1940

Mercer, F. A. and Gaunt, W.
POSTER PROGRESS
The Studio Ltd. 1939

Ogg, Oscar
AN ALPHABET SOURCE BOOK
Harper & Brothers 1940

Petrina, John
ART WORK: HOW PRODUCED, HOW REPRODUCED
Pitman Publishing Corp. 1937

Price, Matlack
SO YOU'RE GOING TO BE AN ARTIST!
Watson-Guptill Publications 1939

Richmond, Leonard
THE TECHNIQUE OF THE POSTER
Sir Isaac Pitman & Sons, Ltd. 1933

Surrey, Richard
LAYOUT TECHNIQUE IN ADVERTISING
McGraw-Hill Book Co. 1929

Tannahil, Sallie B.
P'S AND Q'S
Doubleday, Page and Co. 1923

Thompson, Samuel W.
THE SCRIPT LETTER
The Studio Ltd. 1939

Wallace, C.
COMMERCIAL ART
McGraw-Hill Book Co. 1939

Wellington, Duke
THEORY AND PRACTICE OF POSTER ART
Signs of Times Publishing Co. 1934

Welo, Samuel
TRADE MARK AND MONOGRAM SUGGESTIONS
Pitman Publishing Corp. 1937

THREE MONOGRAPHS ON COLOR
International Printing Ink Co. 1935

ANNUALS

Art Director's Annual
Watson-Guptill Publications

Production Yearbook
Colton Press

U. S. Camera
U. S. Camera Publishing Co.

MAGAZINES

A-D Magazine

American Artist

Design

Graphic Arts Monthly

Signs of the Times

BROCHURES

Better Impressions
Mead Paper Corporation

Design and Paper
Marquardt Paper Company

Westvaco Inspirations for Printers
West Virginia Pulp and Paper Company

INDEX

GALLERY OF POSTERS

Courtesy of Museum of Modern Art Steinlen

Courtesy of Museum of Modern Art Lautrec

Courtesy of Museum of Modern Art Cheret

Courtesy of Museum of Modern Art Hohlwein

Courtesy of Museum of Modern Art Herkendell

Courtesy of Museum of Modern Art Cassandre

DU 11 AU 28 AOUT
DANS TOUTE LA FRANCE

"JOURNÉES
D'ESPÉRANCE"

SECRÉTARIAT G^AL. FOYER DE LA PAIX 34 B^D. RASPAIL. PARIS

Carlu

Courtesy of Museum of Modern Art Uher

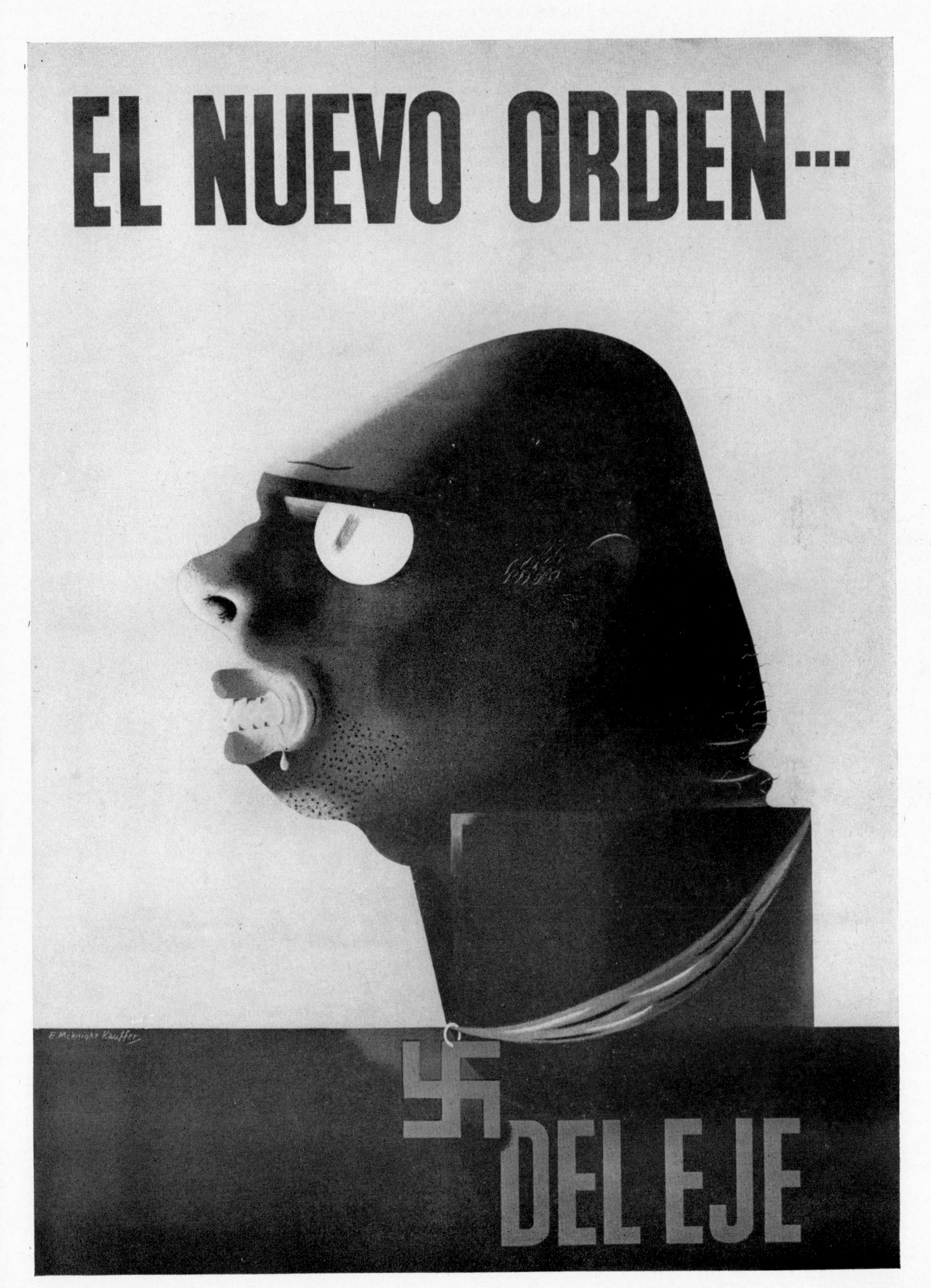

Courtesy of the artist Kauffer

Matter

Dryden

Courtesy of British Ministry of Information Keely

Courtesy of Swiss Consulate of New York

Courtesy of Russian War Relief

Courtesy of British Ministry of Information Keely

Courtesy of Museum of Modern Art Melendreras

Courtesy of the artist Kauffer

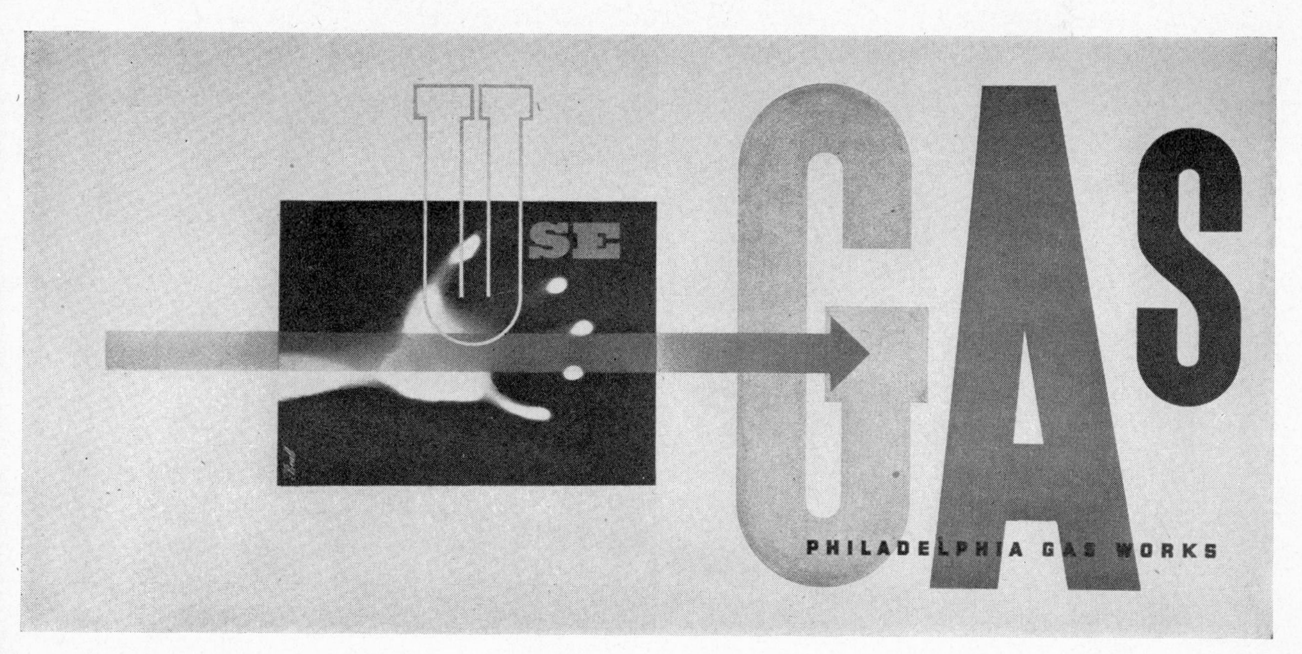

Courtesy of the Artist Beall

Courtesy of Outdoor Advertising, Inc. Johnson and Kerlee

Courtesy of Outdoor Advertising, Inc. Binder

Courtesy of Outdoor Advertising, Inc. Staehle

Courtesy of McCann-Erickson, Inc. Rockwell

Courtesy of the artist

Beall

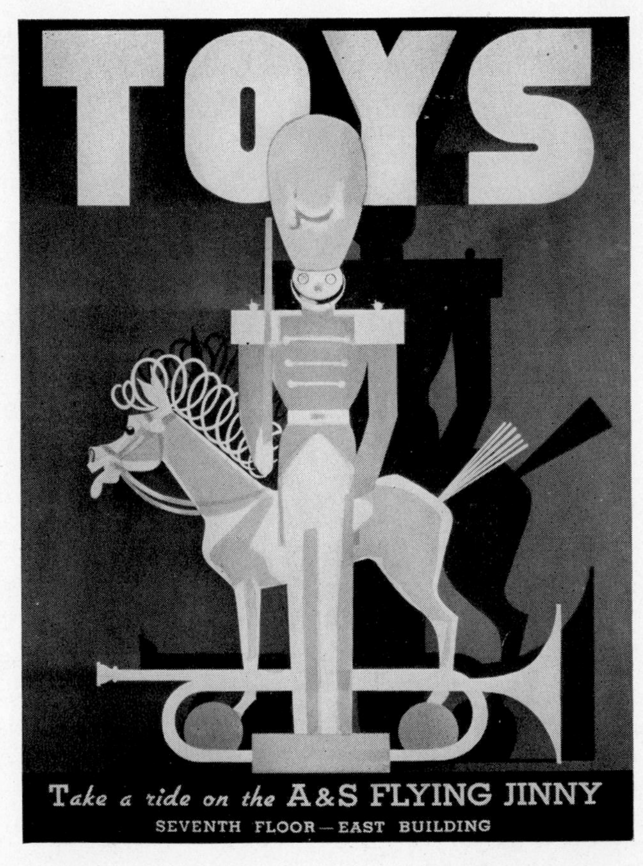

Courtesy of Abraham & Straus

Courtesy of Bloomingdale's

Courtesy of Outdoor Advertising, Inc. Shepard

Watch the
Fords go by
U.S.

Courtesy of Outdoor Advertising Inc. Staehle

Courtesy of Outdoor Advertising Inc. Ryan

Courtesy of Outdoor Advertising, Inc. Bomar

Courtesy of Outdoor Advertising, Inc. MacNutt

Courtesy of Outdoor Advertising Inc. Steig

Courtesy of Outdoor Advertising, Inc. Williams

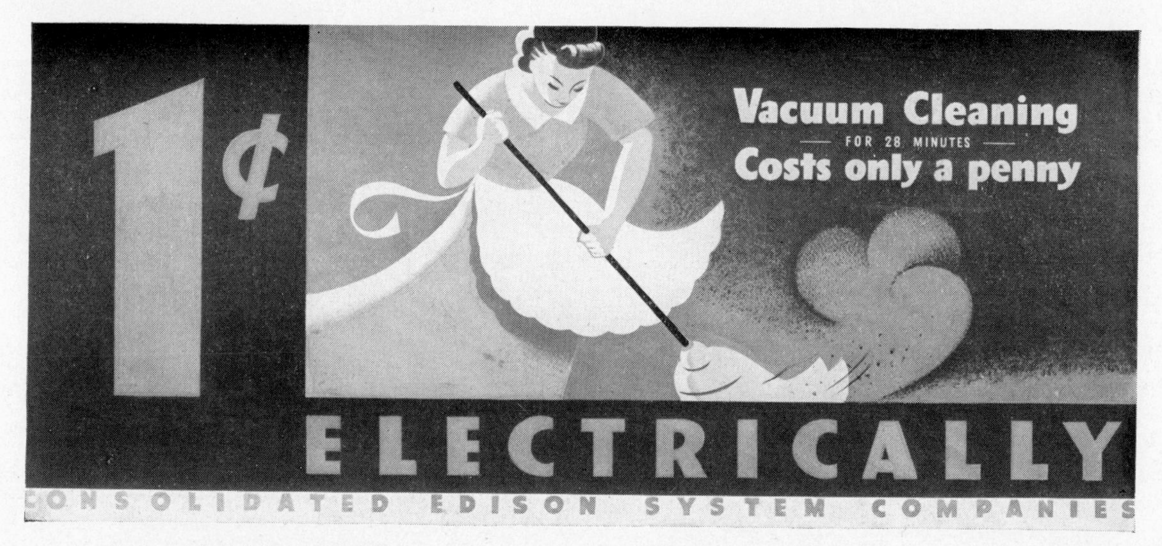

Courtesy of Consolidated Edison Company Seifert

Courtesy of Outdoor Advertising, Inc. De Looy

Courtesy of Outdoor Advertising, Inc. Freenan, Emerson, Powers

Courtesy of American Display Corporation

Courtesy of Southern Pacific Railways

Courtesy of the artist Ragan

Courtesy of the artist Maurer

Courtesy of Southern Pacific Railways

Courtesy of Museum of Modern Art

Kamens

Courtesy of Outdoor Advertising Inc. Binder

Courtesy of Consolidated Edison Co. Staff Artist

Courtesy of Office of War Information Rockwell

HELP A GREEK CHILD

TO SURVIVE

E. McKnight Kauffer

CONTRIBUTE TO FRIENDS OF GREECE INC., 52 EAST 57TH STREET, NEW YORK CITY

Courtesy of the artist Kauffer

a careless word

...another cross

Courtesy of Office of War Information Atherton

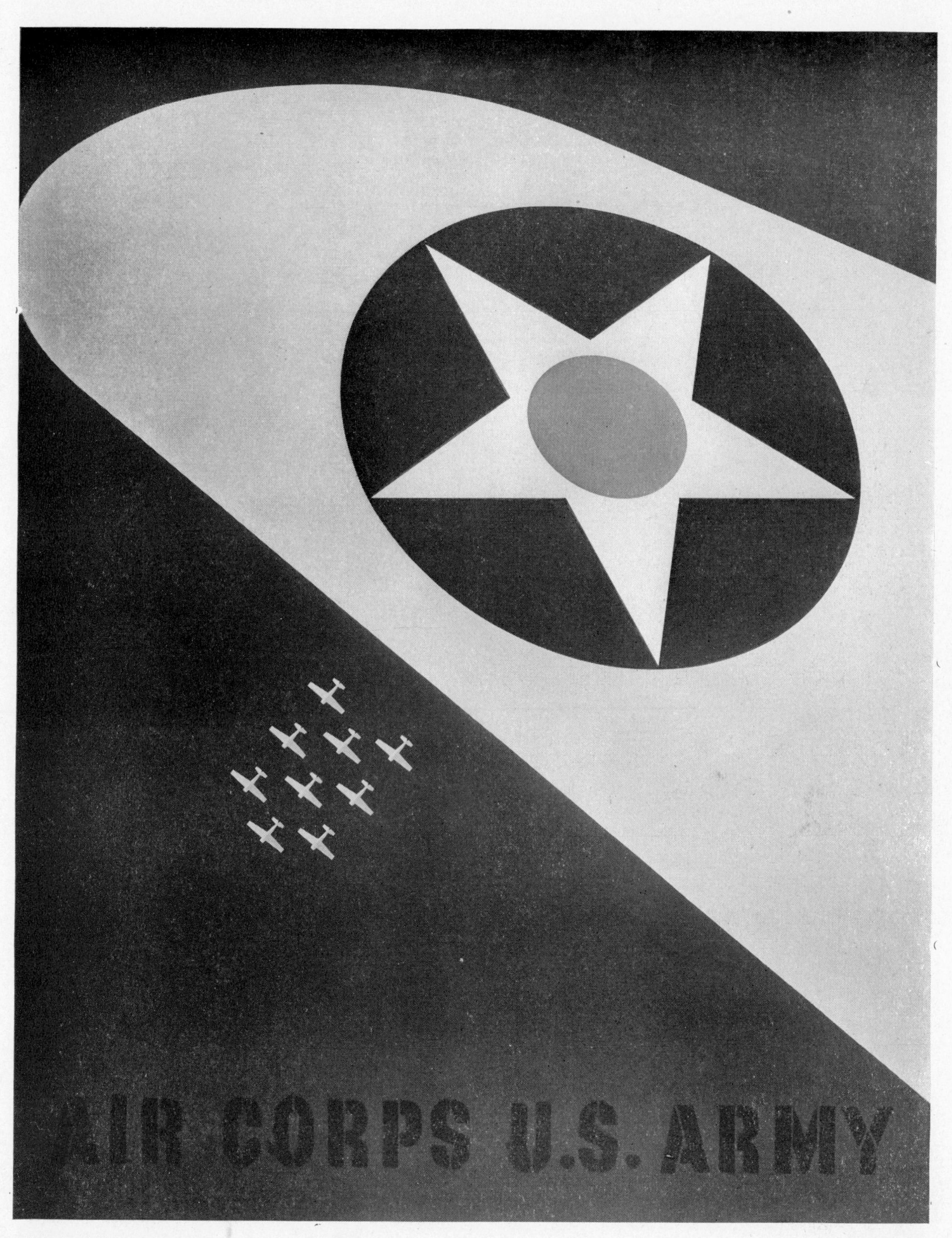

Courtesy of Museum of Modern Art Binder

Courtesy of McCann-Erickson, Inc. Noxon

Courtesy of Outdoor Advertising, Inc. Bernhard

Courtesy of McCann-Erickson, Inc. Hayden

Courtesy of McCann-Erickson, Inc. Scott

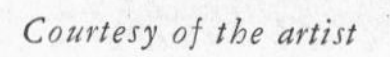

Courtesy of the artist Maurer

Courtesy of Office of War Information Helguera

Courtesy of Office of War Information Hirsch

Courtesy of Office of War Information Atherton

Courtesy of Office of War Information

Courtesy of Office of War Information Dohanos

Courtesy of Office of War Information

Courtesy of Office of War Information Anderson

Courtesy of the artist Kauffer